Greatness is not measured by what
a man or woman accomplishes,
but by the opposition he or she
has overcome to reach that goal.

— Dorothy Height —

When at a young age you learn to
face fears, that makes the difference
between people being champions
and people not being champions.

— Abbas Karimi —

WHAT PEOPLE ARE SAYING ABOUT ABBAS AND **THIS GIFT:**

"

Beneath Abbas's humility, his politeness and boyish charms, is a bottomless reserve of grit and steel. How else to explain the extraordinary arc of his young life? You would be hard-pressed to come up with a more unlikely story. Born armless, in the midst of conflict, in one of the poorest nations on earth, Abbas leaves home, becomes a refugee, travels halfway across the world, and somehow ends up representing his birthplace before the whole world in the Tokyo Paralympic Games. Abbas has shown us all what human will is capable of. He is an inspiration to anybody with a dream and obstacles lying in the path to it. Whenever I think of him, what he has accomplished, everything seems a little more possible. He is one of my heroes.

Khaled Hosseini
Award-winning author of The Kite Runner, And the Mountains Echoed, Sea Prayer, *and* A Thousand Splendid Suns

Anita called me and said there was an armless swimmer from Afghanistan at the Swim Fort Lauderdale practices, and I knew there was a story there. But Abbas's story was more inspiring than I could have ever imagined. When I got to the pool to do the story, I was first impressed by his physical ability and how much faster he was than all the other swimmers. But when we talked, I realized it was his journey that was most inspiring of all. When we started the interview, Abbas put the microphone on with his foot, and I knew in that moment: this guy can do anything. I'll never forget his positive attitude. I can't wait to see what comes next for him.

Brian Entin
Senior Reporter, WGN NewsNation

We are fortunate to have Abbas as a UNHCR Ambassador. He has the power to inspire and when you meet Abbas, that is what you notice before you realize that he does not have arms.

Claire Lewis
United Nations High Commissioner for Refugees (UNHCR)

Everyone has challenges. Ours are just packaged differently. No one's life is perfect. Abbas's challenge is just very obvious. And life goes on. He is making the most of it. He is the definition of a true champion. There are not enough awards for what he has done.

Marty Hendrick
Head Coach, SFTL Masters; Coach, Tokyo 2020 Refugee Paralympic Team; Coach, 2010, 2014, 2015, 2016, 2017, and 2021 US Masters Swimming Club National Champions; Coach, 2015 US Masters Swimming Club of the Year

I think the word 'inspirational' is probably overused. But meeting Abbas Karimi for the first time, I immediately knew he might as well be the dictionary definition of it. Watching this young athlete rocket through the pool, put on a mask with his feet, and text using his toes would all be incredible for someone born with the resources available in America. But Abbas, of course, wasn't born here. This refugee did it the really (really) hard way. And his journey— from growing up in Afghanistan to ending up training in Fort Lauderdale for the Paralympics—is a testament to his pure grit and determination. I later heard Abbas tell his story to a small group— and it hit me that he's not anywhere close to a polished motivational speaker. But he is, without a doubt, a motivational human being.

Daniel Cohen
WSVN-7 News Miami producer whose team won a 2021 regional Emmy for their story about Abbas

Maybe Abbas would have stayed with my team, Oregon Reign Masters, had the pandemic not shut down all the pools. I hated to let him go. My love for Abbas is big, and that is why I told him he had to go to Fort Lauderdale where the outdoor pools were open. When you really love someone, it is not hard to let them go. You want what is best for them.

Dennis Baker
Head Coach, Oregon Reign Masters; two-time Olympic finalist in the 200 butterfly, with seven world records at the masters level

As coaches, this is our job—to deal with the bad things that happen to the athletes…because those things affect how they swim. What they eat, how they sleep, how much they rest, and what else is going on in their lives all matters. You say you will not think about it and that you will focus on the race, but we all have our limits. Most of all, it depends on the combination of those things on the day they are competing. Not every race is the same.

Coach Alexander Tsoltos
Olympic swimmer, 2004 Athens; Paralympic Coach for Ibrahim Al Hussein (Syria)

Copyright © 2024 by Anita Mitchell

All rights reserved. No part of this book may be reproduced or transmitted in any form or by any means, electronic or mechanical, including: photocopying, recording, or by any information storage and retrieval system, without permission in writing from the copyright owner.
This work is based on the experiences of an individual. Every effort has been made to ensure the accuracy of the content.

This Gift: The Story of Abbas Karimi, PLY

Author: Anita Mitchell
Associate Editor: Griffin Mill
Proofreaders: Lyda Rose Haerle, Pipa Aldoro
Art Direction: Anita Mitchell
Cover Design: Nicole Wurtele
Cover Photo: Madison Nicole Yelle; Madison Nicole Photography
Interior Layout: Michael Nicloy

ISBN: 979-8-9881891-5-2

PUBLISHED BY CG SPORTS PUBLISHING

AN IMPRINT OF
NICO 11 PUBLISHING & DESIGN
MUKWONAGO, WISCONSIN
MICHAEL NICLOY, PUBLISHER
www.nico11publishing.com

Quantity order requests can be emailed to:
mike@nico11publishing.com

Printed in The United States of America

There is no shortcut to any place worth going.

Anita Mitchell

Good enough has never been good enough

God Took My Arms, but He Gave Me
THIS GIFT
The Story of Abbas Karimi, PLY

By Anita Mitchell

Your strength doesn't come from winning.
It comes from struggles and hardship.
Everything that you go through
prepares you for the next level.

— Germany Kent —

It doesn't matter if you look different.
You're still the same as everybody else
because you have the same dream.

— Natalie du Toit —

South African swimmer

FOREWORD
Abbas Karimi

Be water
Empty your mind
Be formless, shapeless, like water
You put water into a cup
it becomes the cup
You put water into a bottle,
it becomes the bottle
You put it into a teapot,
it becomes the teapot
Now water can flow or it can crash
Be water, my friend
— Bruce Lee —

Abbas at Bruce Lee's grave.

I was born without arms. People from around Kabul would come watch me swim when I was thirteen. I started to compete and dreamed of becoming an elite athlete. But to do so, I had to leave behind my home and my family in Kabul. With the help of my older brother, I flew to Tehran, Iran, where my brother arranged for smugglers to take me across the Turkish border.

For three days and three nights I was cold, hungry, and scared. Had I been caught, at best I would have been sent back to Afghanistan. At worst I may have been raped, tortured, or killed.

After days of hiding in the back of a truck with twenty other people, I crossed the border into Turkey.

I lived in Turkey for four years, in four different refugee camps. I had no documentation, no passport, no country. I convinced the people at the first refugee camp to take me to a pool where I could swim. For eight months I rode a bus for an hour each way to swim in the morning. I returned to the refugee camp for lunch, then did it again in the afternoon. That is four hours per day on a bus.

I missed my family terribly. Many times I questioned my decision to leave Kabul to chase this dream.

I was constantly on social media posting videos of myself swimming and talking about my wish to leave Turkey and go to a country that would support my goals. Mike Ives saw my video and became my Facebook friend. In 2015, Mike petitioned the United Nations High Commissioner (UNHCR) for Refugees to let me come to the United States.

After months of interviews and applications, I got to Portland, only to soon face the closing of the pools because of the pandemic.

I had nowhere to swim and I was losing valuable training time.

The outdoor pools in Fort Lauderdale, Florida, were open, and a Portland swimmer knew of a Fort Lauderdale masters swim team. I came to train with Swim Fort Lauderdale, and live with Coach Marty Hendrick.

I made the 2020 Tokyo Paralympic team as a refugee athlete.

On August 27, 2021, I competed in the 50-meter butterfly in Tokyo as a Paralympian. On that same day, the Taliban seized Kabul.

My family was still there.

This is my story.

I was a refugee for ten years. On March 22, 2022, I became an American citizen. Although my application was expedited, it still took years. They needed my fingerprints on the application, and I do not have fingers. Every single thing that I do is complicated. Fingerprints are just a recent example.

Now that I am an American, I am able to train in the Olympic/Paralympic training facility in Colorado Springs. I had to earn this spot, since the number of athletes allowed is limited. I am part of the USA Paralympic team. I get very emotional when I talk about my life. I still cry a lot. I have to get through this part, because it will open the doors for me to inspire others. Mine is not an easy story, but it needs to be told. I have been both tortured by misfortune and blessed beyond my wildest dreams.

When things become hard for me, I endure. No matter what happens to me, I endure. I believe a tough journey is the only journey. I am grateful every day.

I am strong-willed, and I rarely listened to anyone when I was growing up. I am still this way, and for the most part, it has worked for me. Everything I have, every problem I have overcome, every success—is because of swimming. I will continue swimming for as long as my body can do it.

My father had hoped that I would become active in our local mosque. But he also wanted me to follow my passion. I've needed to be saved so many times but have learned that really the only person who can save me is me.

I am alone on this journey and am learning more about myself all the time. I see myself like this:

Someday, Abbas Karimi will live in the mountains. He will have his own animals to feed, money for whatever he wants, a peaceful, quiet life, and a family of his own. That day will come but first he must become a gold-medal Paralympian.

For every refugee seeking a better life, a new country, a new beginning, I am doing this for you, too. When I am up on that podium, I am going to make all of you happy, everywhere around the world.

DON'T QUIT. SUFFER NOW AND LIVE
THE REST OF YOUR LIFE AS A CHAMPION
— MUHAMMED ALI —

ONE

TODAY IS THE DAY: DREAM CAME TRUE; EXCEPT FOR THIS

*Lose yourself in the music, the moment
You own it, you better never let it go
You only get one shot,
do not miss your chance to blow
This opportunity comes once in a lifetime.*

— Eminem —

from the soundtrack to the movie 8 Mile

In less than 40 seconds, my life was ruined. I was the world's biggest loser. My pride was shattered. My reputation was tarnished. I had let down my coach and all the coaches who came before him. I let my country down, I let my people down, I let every refugee down. I let my father's memory down and I let the rest of my family down. I let my body down. My face had the look of pure rage. I was like a person who never even made the Tokyo Paralympic team. I was with them. I should have done better but I didn't.

When I got out of the water...I was so angry...everyone wanted to talk to me...after all, I was the only Afghan refugee at the Paralympics while the Taliban was seizing control of Kabul, the biggest news story in the whole world. Everybody wanted to talk to me, NBC, CNN, New York Times, BBC...I had given my word that I would talk to them, that was part of the deal...I signed a contract promising that I would talk to them...but I spoke with no reporters...Instead, I just kept

walking…my coach expected me to do the interviews but today I could not live up to his standards.
My family was messaging me on Facebook all day long.
…I went to the cool down pool to recover from the swim then me and my shattered heart went back to the Olympic village.

I did this to myself, it was my own fault. I was thinking about my family and my country, I was not 100 percent there. I screwed up. I cried and cried. Then I cried more. My father used to tell me what to do and I did not listen. Even if people tell me the right things, I don't listen but I also don't regret that I don't listen. Failing is good. You learn from that. We fail; we fall down from the ladder, which is what success is; it is a hard thing yet it is also a very attractive mindset. Maybe it is not the best way to do things, but it has worked for me. This way of thinking is how I made it so far.

I am a tough guy. I feel good about my decisions even if they are the wrong decisions. I control my own life and what I do. Today it did not work out.

I am one of the millions who fled the violence in Afghanistan long before the current crisis. Because of the chaos surrounding the Taliban takeover and the U.S. withdrawal, Afghanistan's Paralympic delegation did not fly to Tokyo. I was the only Afghan athlete to compete at the Games.
Afghanistan's Paralympic committee officially said they were "unable to compete" in the wake of the Taliban's return to power.
The team, made up of just two taekwondo athletes, has since been evacuated from Afghanistan though officials have declined to say where they ended up.

It started like this:

It was August 27, 2021, the final 50-meter butterfly. The Paralympic Games is the largest international event for disabled athletes and takes place shortly after every Olympic Games in the same host city. The Games are held every four years and these were the summer games. The prelims were in the morning and now I was back at the Tokyo Aquatic Centre, the nearly $400 million pool built especially for the 2020 Olympics. The arena can accommodate an audience of 12,000 but was virtually empty because of the global pandemic.

First, second, and third place swimmers would get the gold, silver, and bronze medals. The picture of me being right here has lived in my mind for as long as I can remember, and like always, I prayed before my races.

Me, Abbas Karimi, at the Paralympic games, competing with swimmers just like me who have different variations of missing limbs. Some have lost limbs because of accidents, some have partial limbs, and others were born without limbs, like I was.

At the same time, the Taliban was taking over Kabul, my childhood home and where 15 of my family members still live. My mind is half on the 50-meter butterfly and half on my family in Kabul.

I came out of the call room where swimmers wait their turn to be escorted to the starting blocks. This is where suits and goggles are adjusted. I got up on the Lane 2 diving block. My coach was with me, I was listening to the theme from the 1984 Sci-Fi classic, *The Terminator*. He removed my headphones and my protective mask.

In Lane 1 was Daniel Dias from Brazil. He was born without hands. His right arm stops at his elbow, while his left arm is also shorter and has just a single finger. His right leg finishes at his knee and he has no feet.

In Lane 3 was Yaruslav Semenenko from Ukraine. Both of his hands were amputated when he was a child after he touched a 6,000 volt transformer.

We are classified as S5 athletes which means we are swimmers with coordination issues or movement problems in the trunk and legs or absence of limbs. Some of us have difficulty swimming straight or holding a good body position.

For me, it is hard for me to swim with my whole body and I must rely heavily on my legs and my flexibility.

I don't remember my dive in or the temperature of the water after the start gun. My right leg hurt and I didn't really feel well. My Arena swimsuit felt tight and I had to pee. My muscles weren't even fully awake, not fully there. My focus didn't have its necessary razor sharpness and The Beast that normally lives within me was somewhere else.

At the same time was a deadly terrorist bomb blast attack at one of the gates in the Hamid Karzai International Airport. There were concerns that another terror attack in Kabul was likely, but maximum force protection measures at the Kabul Airport were being taken. The death toll there increased to more than 170 people killed and 200 wounded from yesterday's Kabul attack.

My brother has been sending me cellphone videos of what is going there. Some people who could not board the planes had climbed and hung from the wings. When the plane took off, they instantly fell to their deaths. My family was there with thousands of other people waiting to get on a plane. Their original plan was to fly from Kabul to Doha, a six hour flight.

When they heard the gunfire, they left and boarded a bus for an 8-hour trip to Pakistan. My brother was making the arrangements. I knew that he had some money which was going to help. I kept checking Facebook Messenger for messages from my brother and he kept reassuring me that everyone was ok. I spoke to him the day of the finals and I was crying at the finals. My biggest fear was that my family was going to be killed or captured. The main thing was for

them to get across the border into Pakistan.
I pray three times a day: In the early morning, in the afternoon, and at night. I prayed a lot in Tokyo. I prayed for Afghanistan, I prayed for my family, I prayed for myself. It was very hard for me to rein it all in.
Today I prayed for the 50-meter butterfly. I needed all the prayer I could get.

TEN METERS INTO THE RACE: I just didn't feel well. I felt pain in my chest, legs, pain everywhere.

It had been nine hours since the preliminary competitions. Earlier today, I had finished third in the prelims where I swam my fastest time, 36.36 seconds. I was a third place finisher and qualified for the finals. Every media outlet wanted to talk to me.

In the back of my mind I knew that at any time they could be captured or killed. I was helpless. My people were suffering, hungry, scared. The Taliban was now controlling Kabul. They had a particular hate for my Hazara tribe.

Just a few hours ago, I was swimming my best. Now I felt as if I were swimming through syrup. Only a few hours ago, my coach and I were ecstatic. I felt great, as if I were flying. It was a whirlwind. I dropped a second and a half off my time. I knew that I did well. My coach was excited too and for nearly five minutes we were on top of the world. After the morning race I was so thirsty. NBC was there to interview me, and I didn't want to do the interview then because I was thirsty and out of breath. The Beast inside of me was exhilarated and thumping his chest. Just a few hours ago, I was soaring.

25 METERS INTO THE RACE: My entire body ached and I saw swimmers pulling ahead.

10 METERS LEFT IN THE RACE: During the race I saw the Brazilian Daniel Dias beating me. I knew that I was going to lose.

I got 8th, last place. 38 seconds. Eternity.

President Ashraf Ghani had already abandoned Afghanistan and fled to Dubai; he denied taking millions of dollars on the way out. The Afghan army had surrendered, and now the Taliban was totally in control.
My Hazara tribe is considered to be one of the most persecuted in the world. The Taliban sees us as infidels. The Hazara ethnic and religious population is especially at high risk and there is a long history of genocide to prove it. As one of the largest ethnic groups in Afghanistan, the Hazara people have endured various forms of oppression from Pashtun rulers and governments, including slavery, systematic expulsion from ancestral homes and lands, and massacres.
My Hazara family could not think about my 50-meter butterfly race. They had to focus on getting out of Afghanistan.

The three Chinese swimmers took 1st, 2nd, and 3rd. Zheng Tao won gold with a world record time at 30.62. He had just dropped his 30-hour 6 days a week training, to 9 hours a week training. He lost both of his arms in an electrical accident when he was a kid. Lichao Wang won silver. He swims six hours a day with a distance of 5k a day. He lost his arms touching electrical wires. Yuan Weiyi is a superstitious swimmer with exact routines and music before he swims. He lost his arms at age eight from an electric shock.

A crowd of local and foreign civilians fled to the airport to be evacuated. At Abbey Gate, one of the gates into the airport, a suicide bomber detonated an explosive belt. After the explosion, gunfire erupted and all gates to the airport were closed.
The United Nations Security Council condemned "in the strongest terms" the deadly attack near the airport in Kabul. My brother had a friend for my family to stay with once they crossed the border to Pakistan. I don't want to say where. I am still protective of their safety. I felt helpless.

AFTERMATH OF THE 50 FLY

After the race, I could not stop sobbing. I had planned this to be my finest moment but when that didn't happen, The Beast roared inside of me. The Beast is always there, I am able to manage it. Today The Beast reared its ugly head for the whole world to see.

People started to restrict me and tell me what to do, something that never works for me. I screamed, "This is my life!!!!."

I was already coached by the UNHCR for interviews and told things like, "Don't use the word smuggled, we don't want people to think they have to pay to flee, instead use the word *journey* and say being in the mountains in the dark and cold was scary, dangerous, and challenging. Say that my father's death was sad but do not say you came back to Kabul to the funeral. Do not talk about politics. If you are asked about being a Hazara, refer to yourself as an Afghan instead of talking about your ethnicity."

I was mentally suffering and I could feel myself losing control. The tears would not stop. I was having a meltdown. I was ready to fight, and I was bombarded by reporters. I was crying so hard when I called my family to apologize to them for losing my competition.

Megumi Aoyama from the UNHCR stepped in and firmly told reporters there were to be no more interviews with me right now.

She made me feel comfortable and was so nice to me, I think I fell in love with her that day. I wanted her around me. She was exactly what I needed at that time. Before we left Tokyo, I went shopping for a gift for her. I love the relaxed feeling I get from girls and beautiful women like her. I have a burning desire for that feeling. Women like her ease my mind.

TEDDY KATZ
Media Attaché for the Refugee Paralympic Team

My job was media attaché for the Refugee Paralympic Team, helping share stories with the world's media in the lead up to and during the Games. I was involved in helping the small support team around these athletes in every way possible including with a lot of logistics—figuring out translation and other obstacles. I had to help build a cohesive team environment in a short period of time. You have to remember, this wasn't your normal team—athletes were coming together from different parts of the world, different cultures, languages, different disabilities.

I have had a lot of experience over the years working as a journalist at dozens of Olympics and Paralympics and serving on the organizing committee of major games, so I knew how you had to prepare for every possible scenario. That really helped when we faced a lot of the things in Tokyo that suddenly surfaced.

With Abbas and many other athletes, we arranged a whole slew of media interviews in the lead up with many of the top media outlets in the US, Europe, Japan, and elsewhere—then I was by their side most time at the Games

*August 27, 2021, the day of the 50-meter butterfly finals: Abbas was dealing with the biggest media story imaginable, a combo platter of the Paralympic games, the Taliban taking over Kabul, an Afghan refugee athlete getting ready for the 50-meter butterfly of his life, and a pandemic.

This is how I helped put that together:

The team had prepared for many different scenarios with COVID-19 and keeping everyone safe as the first priority.

The refugee Paralympic team had six athletes representing millions of refugees and displaced people from around the world.

One lived in a refugee camp in Rwanda, others were in Greece, one in Germany, two in the US.

We had to get them and their coaches to pre-Games events to qualify for the Games.

We felt we won a medal just getting everybody to Tokyo safely under those circumstances and in the middle of the pandemic.

When the games were about to start, the world changed.

Few could have predicted the speed of the changes that occurred in Afghanistan on the eve of the Games.

Those changes put enormous stress on one of our athletes, Abbas Karimi, as he was one of the faces of the team. He was one of two members of the team going to carry the Paralympic flag into the Opening Ceremonies. He was also one of the only athletes from Afghanistan in Tokyo. Suddenly every media organization from around the world sent me messages. They all wanted to interview Abbas. It was a firestorm that few athletes in their mid-20s have ever had to deal with. Suddenly, he was worried about his friends and family while somehow trying to maintain his focus at his first ever Paralympics—something he had dreamed about in his darkest moments—his dream was finally becoming a reality but not the way he envisioned it.

It was a stressful time for everybody on the team including me. We were concerned about Abbas' mental health and wellbeing— you can only imagine how much this was all weighing on his shoulders.

He went to Tokyo with a goal to get on the podium. Suddenly, he had other much bigger concerns—nobody knew what was going to happen back in his birth country.

We tried to ease the burden as much as we could. We were due to host a news conference introducing the team to the world's media just before the opening ceremony. We knew Abbas was in high demand from the media. He was one of the only athletes on the team who spoke English, and we offered him the choice to decide if he wanted to come with the team to that news conference. We wanted it to be his choice—we were concerned about his mental wellness. When he decided not to attend, I knew it was the right thing to do. I breathed a sigh of relief.

The media all wanted to speak to Abbas about his views on what was happening in Afghanistan. He couldn't really speak about that—but some media were very persistent. They sent e-mails—many showed up to his races. When we explained he wasn't comfortable speaking about the political situation in Afghanistan, that he wanted to try to keep his focus on why he was in Tokyo—to perform at his first Paralympics—most media were very understanding.

They understood that he was at his first games—trying to keep his focus on his goal of winning a medal—despite everything going on around him.

The morning of the 50 fly went as well as it could have under those circumstances. Abbas swam the race of his life without anything holding him back—his first Paralympic race and he swam faster than he ever did before to qualify for the final.

He was ecstatic and told the media, in what is known as the mixed zone, there was more to come that night—that this race put him in a good position to achieve his dream of getting on the podium.

I'm not too sure what happened after that. Maybe he didn't relax the way he normally does in the hours between that race and the final. Marty, his coach, tells me he didn't rest the way he needed to—maybe he started thinking about the result too much rather than doing everything the way he did that morning.

In any case, that morning he looked like he was swimming effortlessly. The evening final didn't go as planned. So it was a 24-hour period with a whirlwind of emotions for Abbas. He didn't have the result he wanted in the final, finishing 8th, not swimming the way he had that morning. He rushed past the media that night not wanting to speak to anybody, needing time to process what had just happened.

Abbas handled the situation as best anybody could in that situation. He was in his 20's sometimes being asked to speak for everyone in Afghanistan. It was an enormous burden for him to carry on his shoulders.

When he was disappointed after not having the result in the 50 M fly final, he was so upset, he didn't want to speak to the media gathered to interview him in the mixed zone. Marty, his coach kept trying to remind him that he was representing 85 million displaced (up to 100 million because of the war in Ukraine and now an estimated 117 million because of the earthquake in Turkey) around the world—as a reminder that he was swimming for a lot more people than just himself.

Abbas had an incredible drive, resilience, and a hunger to perform like few athletes I've ever seen before. I've covered a lot of athletes in 20 years as a sports journalist. Abbas was unique in many ways. It was as if he was trying to show the world nothing could stop him. Many things could have gotten in his way of getting to Tokyo. From being bullied as a child, to having to escape violence in his country, to being isolated from his family.

His journey was full of hurdles that would have stopped most of us dead in our tracks. Not Abbas. Tokyo was another microcosm of his life story.

He had moments of incredible highs followed by incredible lows. I have no doubt we will see him on a Paralympic podium one day soon and his Tokyo experience he'll say was the catalyst—where he learned another important lesson about how he can get through anything.

In 1992, I was living in Barcelona for the unforgettable Olympics and Paralympics.

I was a reporter for Canada, covering one of the biggest stories about a world champion rower making a miraculous recovery from injury to win a bronze medal. This athlete had her leg nearly shattered by a German boat because of an accident in training two months before the Games and practically had to be lifted into the boat to win a bronze medal. She became a household name in Canada.

When the Olympics ended, I was the only journalist there from Canada covering the Paralympics and meeting 300 athletes there, with stories equally as powerful as that Olympic rower. It became one of my passions to try to tell those Paralympic stories around the world. Being the media attaché and working with refugee athletes was a dream job. Being able to share Abbas' and the others' stories was the epitome of the kind of storytelling that makes me jump out of bed in the morning. There are so many lessons in all of their stories.

Abbas could teach a master class on the drive to carry on and to overcome adversity. He likes to refer to himself as The Lion, and like The Lion, he is a symbol of courage and extraordinary strength."

HERE IS WHAT HAPPENED DURING THE NINE HOURS BEFORE THE 50 FLY FINALS:

There were nine hours between the end of the prelims and the finals. It was crucial that I relax. I chatted with an Afghan friend in Portland, Oregon. Maybe I talked to my brother and got a family update, but I really don't remember. The data on my phone was turned off so I didn't know what was going on in Afghanistan.

The idea of relaxing is not a strong enough concept for what I needed. I was crying a lot. I did not simply need to just relax. I needed to completely shut down and shut it all off, my family, what was going on in Afghanistan, my swimming, everything. I needed a break, a total detachment.

Before we even left Fort Lauderdale for Tokyo, my brother was telling me how the Taliban was on their way to Kabul and that they were starting to take over the country. Droves of people were leaving Afghanistan and going to Pakistan, to Iran, to the United Arab Emirates (UAE). I was not surprised that the Taliban had taken over Kabul.

Earlier Thursday, the Taliban sprayed a water cannon at those gathered at one airport gate to try to drive the crowd away, as someone launched tear gas canisters elsewhere. About 4,200 people were evacuated from Kabul on Friday. The evacuations were carried out from 3 a.m. to 3 p.m. By noon, US military flights had evacuated about 2,100 people and 29 coalition flights had also evacuated approximately 2,100 people.
Approximately 7,500 people were evacuated from Kabul over the same 12-hour stretch of time on Thursday. The US had evacuated and facilitated the evacuation of about 109,200 people.

I decided to eat a melatonin gummy bear. You eat them like candy, and they can give relief from anxiety, although everyone has a different reaction. The gummy can make you feel better pretty quickly and can ease the feeling of stress. It can take the edge off of anxiety and promote calmness and tranquility. I was desperate for that. None of that happened for me. It just made me sleep, and I was tired when I awoke.

I told Marty that I ate the gummy. When I ate it, I knew it was a bad choice, but I did it. I have done a lot of wrong things, and I have learned from them.

No one is perfect. I own the mistake as mine. I would not have listened to anyone anyway.

It's just not what I do.

Don't fear failure. Low aim is the crime.
In great attempts, it is glorious even to fail
— Bruce Lee —

TWO
COACH MARTY HENDRICK

> As coaches, it is our job to deal with the bad things that happen to the athletes... because those things affect how they swim. What they eat, how they sleep, how much they rest and what else is going on in their lives all matter. You say you will not think about it and that you will focus on the race but we all have our limits. Most of all, it depends on the combination of those things on the day they are competing.
> Not every race is the same.
>
> *— Coach Alexander Tsoltos —*
> *Olympic swimmer, 2004 Athens.*
> *Paralympic Coach for*
> *Ibrahim Al Hussein from Syria*

Swim Fort Lauderdale (SFTL) head coach Marty Hendrick.

MARTY HENDRICK
Abbas' Coach

I was never angry at Abbas but I was concerned. We had obligations. My frustration came from not even being able to comprehend what was going on in his life. I knew that his family had always wanted him to come back to Afghanistan. Now they were begging him. They were desperate. They left Kabul with what they could carry. This was so far beyond my scope of knowledge, and I could not comprehend what he was going through. They were at the airport, they saw gunfire and left before a suicide bomber killed himself and took down 170 people and 13 military members with him.

I am a smart, corporate-trained, levelheaded guy and I can respond well in an emergency. OK, I am kind of a control freak, but I can always adapt. However, no amount of coach's training had ever prepared me for what I was now going through with

Abbas. I will never fully comprehend his life or understand his life's journey.

I don't fault him for the gummy bear thing. He is a human being complete with shortcomings. Sure, I can say, *how could he do that*, but I really could never understand. As much as I thought I understood him, there are limitations. Thank God we had the morning of the prelims.

Theoretically, I am Abbas' arms, I have to put on his mask, his swimsuit, carry his things, hold his clothes, and sometimes feed him. As flexible, capable and fiercely independent as he is, he still needs help.

I am also his coach. I keep his body on a schedule so that he eats properly and gets all the rest he needs. I orchestrate his workouts. I monitor his progress. I correct his stroke. Unlike the other refugee Paralympic swimmers, he also had qualifying times.

Our schedule on August 27, 2021, the morning of the 50-meter butterfly prelims, went like clockwork. 6:25 a.m. was warm-up swim time, not 6:26 a.m. We are dealing with races that are won or lost in fractions of seconds so the precision part needed to start right here.

There were nine hours between prelims and finals. Although that seems like a lot of time to rest, he was also obligated to do media interviews, eat, and relax before the finals later that day. We had to wear masks at all times and every day we were tested for COVID-19. Had he tested positive, he would not have been allowed to compete.

Each country has its own staff and amenities to help its athletes maintain their peak performances. They have submersion ice tubs, changing areas, massage therapists, nutritionists, physical therapists, and sports psychologists.

Although Abbas is living in the United States, at that time he was not an American citizen: he was a refugee and had none of those things.

He had me.

Abbas is one of six refugee Paralympic athletes whose story attracts massive media attention. The plight of these refugees from around the world are highlighted through the Paralympics. The team consists of athletes from Afghanistan, Burundi, and Iran as well as three from Syria, including swimmer Ibrahim Al Hussein, one of two athletes who formed the first Paralympic refugee team at the 2016 Rio de Janeiro Games.

The one woman and five men will compete in athletics, swimming, canoeing, and Taekwondo.

On the morning of the 50-meter butterfly, Abbas was in total control. He was like a highly focused confident lion. His inner beast was at full throttle, sheer perfection.

During the morning, we watched the time to the second, and I focused on being both a coach and a caretaker. Often I had to combine and switch those roles. Sometimes I did them simultaneously. Before the prelims, I was in the role of swim coach preparing my athlete for an international event. We had tapered his amount of his swimming so that his muscles could relax. There were so many interruptions to our regular routine, the 14-hour time change, checking for COVID-19 every day, having to isolate, losing a day from being stuck in the Dallas airport. Plus, Abbas had commitments to the refugee team and I had coaching meetings. In the call room I was the caretaker, helping him put on his swimsuit and always watching the time. I live by my watch.

Abbas slept well and had a big breakfast at the Olympic Village buffet, eggs, plain yogurt, and watermelon before the 20-minute bus ride to the pool. The food choices were endless with the first section including a salad bar, deli, fruit, and desserts. There was also Chinese cuisine, Asian cuisine, world cuisine, pizzas, pastas—really, anything you can imagine.

That morning of the 50 fly prelims I was 100 percent focused on him and he was focused too. You don't medal from the prelims, you qualify for the finals by getting a 1st, 2nd or 3rd in the prelims. He was in the first heat in lane 7 and came in 3rd so he qualified for the finals. He dropped a second and a half off his seed time to a 36.36.

I was ecstatic. When he walked across the pool area he had the strut of a champion. He would always tell me after competitions that he felt like he was going to die at the end. What keeps him going is his life's journey. This time he got out of the pool and said, "That was easy. It did not hurt at all."

At that point, he was in view of being a medalist, and I was confident that he could do it.

He was ready.

All of the media wanted to talk to him. Abbas had a good chance of winning the medal. All was so good. He even seemed adequately distracted from his family in Kabul and the Taliban headed toward there. He was doing a great job at being distracted. He was excited and ready to swim.

You could feel his inner fire that morning after the swim and during the interview he had with NBC, you could see that he was still out of breath from his swim.

As confident as I was about Abbas, I wrestled with my own feelings of insecurity...was I a good enough coach for this?

Sure, I am a lifelong swimmer with hundreds of awards, top ten national awards and All-American honors but the world stage of the Tokyo Paralympic Games is a whole different level of coaching. Deep within I questioned my coaching abilities. Yes, I had multiple training sessions and years of experience. I had already coached another Paralympic athlete, Justin Zook. Zook was born missing half his right foot and had non-functioning growth plates in his right leg; 30 operations lengthened his leg but caused nerve damage, muscle weakness, and motion problems. He started swimming as physical therapy at age six. Justin came to our pool as a gold medalist, made the 2012 London Paralympic team and set a world record in London for the 100 meter backstroke. He also swam in 2004 Athens and 2008 Beijing. Justin is a women's swim coach at St Catherine's College in St. Paul, Minnesota. He joined my masters team after college. I know his parents. He liked to dive off the blocks. It was not part of regular masters practice, but I got one of the lifeguards to set up a block for him on the days he swam.

I have coached many champion swimmers and was the 2015 Speedo/U.S. Masters Swimming Coach of the Year. I also have the 2011 Kerry O'Brien Coaching Award. I was the Honorary Speaker at the 2014 American Swim Coaches Association (ASCA) World Wide Conference, was inducted into the Broward County Sports Hall of Fame, created a city-wide swim program in Fort Lauderdale with 22 choices of practices a week, I served as a US Masters Convention Delegate, am a member of the USMS Coaches Committee. I am currently the Chair of the Florida Gold Coast LMSC, and a member of the Diversity Task Force for US Masters Swimming.

As a USMS Swimmer, I have multiple Masters FINA World Top 10 rankings, 52 individual and 82 relay USMS National Top 10 rankings, and still have the USMS National record as a member of the 4 X 10,000 relay (Mixed 55+ Age Group). In my tenure coaching Masters Swimmers, I have coached 63 USMS Individual All-Americans, 170 USMS Relay All-Americans with over 230 Individual National Championship swims. My teams have also achieved success at the International level by winning two IGLA Small Team Titles in 2008 and 2011 as well as a Top 10 performance at the 2009 Pan American Championships in Vera Cruz, Mexico.

Swim Fort Lauderdale, our masters swim team, has won five national championships. I am a certified American Swim Coaches Association (ASCA) USMS (U.S. Masters Swimming) Level 4 Coach (one of the first 14 in USMS), and have been coaching at the Fort Lauderdale Aquatic Complex full time since 2005.

But still, was I good enough for this?

THE NIGHT BEFORE THE MORNING OF THE 50 FLY PRELIMS, THE REST PERIOD, AND THEN, THE FINALS:

Under the shiny surface, hell was breaking loose.

On the night before the 50 fly, all of Abbas's family were trying to get into Pakistan, and we were trying to wire them $3,000. His family was facing a dangerous situation and they were begging for help. They had left the Kabul airport when they saw and heard gunfire, just before the suicide bomber exploded. We found someone to wire money to them. I thought a big chunk of the problem was solved

ISIS in Khorasan, known as ISIS-K, has claimed responsibility for the airport attack. It was a lone suicide bomber that was responsible for the airport blast that killed over 170 Afghans, 13 US service members, and injured many more. A single explosive device sent ball bearings through a packed crowd. US troops were wearing protective body armor and helmets, but there was nothing to prevent catastrophic injuries to uncovered areas.

Investigators said the blast was the work of a single ISIS terrorist who was dressed in black and outfitted with an improvised explosive device that had an estimated 20 pounds of explosives.

The force of the ball bearings were so severe, they initially appeared to be gunshot wounds.

Video and eyewitness reports later confirmed that although the wounds looked like gunshots, they were ball bearings; another example of how the battlefield is often a confusing and contradictory place.

Every media outlet wanted to talk to Abbas. The Paralympic story was now also the Afghanistan story. There were lists of people who wanted to talk to us. We were warned by our media liaison about the aggressive New York Times reporter. She wanted to know about his being part of the Hazara tribe, and we did not want dangerous exposure to his name. The reporter clearly only cared about filing a good story. She tried to trick Abbas into answering things that could have harmed both him and his family. I refused to talk to the Times reporter because she was rude to Abbas, but I finally agreed to talk to her.

After his cooldown swim, we took the bus back to the Olympic Village for lunch and rest. I needed to attend the daily coaches meeting. He turned off his phone data so he did not know what was going on in Afghanistan. I went to the meeting, and when I returned from the meeting, Abbas told me that the Pakistani guy we had been trying to send money to got in trouble and Abbas's family never got the money that we were trying to send.

Then he told me that he swallowed a melatonin gummy bear. I did not know what to do. When I travel internationally, I take a sleeping pill on the plane; then when I arrive in my new time zone, I take a melatonin gummy bear at night. These are not CBD-infused or prescription gummy bears. I get a big bottle of them for $9.99 at CVS pharmacy. They are fine to relax and sleep but not to prepare for the swim race of your life.

In hindsight, maybe I should have pumped him full of coffee. I was not really worried about melatonin. Abbas simply had too much on his shoulders.

THE FINALS OF THE 50-METER BUTTERFLY: THE CULMINATION OF TRAINING FOR NINE YEARS STARTED OUT LIKE THIS:

While we were being escorted to the pool, Abbas was void. Even when he told me about the money not getting to his family, he was visually blank. I saw nothing there in his eyes.

We worked on stretching, drinking fluids, and our usual routine of bathroom, five minutes for prayer, breakfast, then swim. Maybe being on autopilot would help. In the afternoon, he was starting to get a little cranky. I kept him structured. Oddly, I could not get the Arena swimsuit on him. It was tight. I had to do everything for him, it was like dressing a spineless mannequin.

He did the warm-up but it was mechanical. He was not cranky, no bravado, no beast, nothing. I didn't see this as a problem. I figured that during warm-up in the cold water, he would be fine. He swam ok, but he was drained of every emotion. He wasn't angry or sad, he was just not there.

At this point I got a little panicky. These nine years could not be gone. We went to the call room on time. The fan was on to assuage the 94-degree heat and humidity. This is the ready room. This is the place to size up the competition. He did not do that. He was void. He had no emotion, no raging beast, no roaring lion. It was almost as if he had a stroke. I wanted to block out everything around him.

When he took off from the dive block, the dive was ok, but the next nearly 40 seconds were a blur to me and I saw that he got 8th, last place.

Abbas got out of the pool in a raging fury. He was devastated, lashing out, and refusing to fulfill his media obligations. We really butted heads. He simply blew up and bolted to the end. "Abbas ,you have to talk to the media for the 82 million refugees," I said, but that did not persuade him.

I did not know what to do. He was shattered. I was numb. Frozen. *What was I thinking? What the fuck am I supposed to do?*

Sources told Al Jazeera that tens of thousands of people had been waiting outside the Abbey Gate earlier in the day. The explosions came after US officials and allies had warned people not to come to the area around Hamid Karzai International due to the threat of an attack.

Several countries urged people to avoid the airport earlier in the day, with one saying there was a threat of a bombing. But just days—or even hours for some nations—before the evacuation effort ended, few appeared to heed the call.

Overnight, warnings emerged from Western capitals about a threat from Afghanistan's ISIL group affiliate, which likely had seen its ranks boosted by the Taliban's freeing of prisoners during their blitz across the country.

British Armed Forces Minister James Heappey told the BBC early Thursday there was "very, very credible reporting of an imminent attack" at the airport, possibly within "hours."

ABBAS, THE NEXT DAY:

> AS ATHLETES WE HAVE UPS AND DOWNS. UNFORTUNATELY, YOU CAN'T PICK THE DAYS THEY COME ON…
>
> — DEANNA KASTORT —
>
> OLYMPIC BRONZE MEDALIST, WOMEN'S MARATHON, 2004 ATHENS GREECE

On the next day, August 28, my face and my story were everywhere. Marty had pretty much stopped talking to me. All I could think about was that my family was in danger, they are suffering and my people are being killed. It seemed so trivial to me that Marty was so bent on following some agreement about giving interviews. I was afraid that this was going to be the end of our relationship. I told him that if he was mad then just be mad and that this would be our last competition together. He was ignoring me.

Everyone wanted to talk to me. My face was out there more than anyone's. A British reporter irritated me when he interviewed me. Here it was less than 24 hours after the 50 fly finals disappointment and this reporter asking me to do a walk and talk interview out in the 94 degree heat. It was all so fake and I hated it. Media people are generally nice and interested in me. They have put my story out there and have been huge supporters of my goal. They often ask me hard questions that affect me emotionally but I understand that they have their story to do. I wanted to be like the other athletes but I wasn't, the focus was on me, they made me so important because of three things: I am an Afghan, my country is being taken over and my family is still there.

COACH MARTY'S FEELINGS ABOUT ABBAS

I really didn't understand what Abbas was going through. Yes, I knew that Afghanistan was riddled with political problems and that his family was there, but I thought that he had his emotions under control. I believed he could separate it.

I underestimated the severity of it all.

I never doubted Abbas's abilities and goals. Abbas talks a big talk. He is confident, he boasts about his goals, he does not doubt himself. For nine years he has been working on this, and at prelims, I believed he was going to medal. There was no question that he could have achieved that goal that evening.

I get frustrated with him because he can be a brat, sort of like a little brother who refuses to listen then gets in the way, but I'm always amazed by him. His authenticity is genuine, and he attracts tremendous support, never out of sympathy, but out of people who admire him. His fellow athletes are also his big supporters.

I am frustrated that he did not have what the other countries had. Had he already received his American citizenship and was part of Team USA with all of the accoutrements it provides, maybe that would have made a difference.

I was never angry at Abbas, but I did feel his disappointment. He is always able to turn it on, and I expected him to do that this time too, but he couldn't.

Abbas will benefit from the specialized training at the Colorado Springs Paralympic training center from former Paralympian Erin Popovich. He is a perfect candidate, and when he gets his American citizenship, he has been accepted to go there. That said, he will always have a home to return to in Fort Lauderdale.

THREE

THE THRILL OF COMING TO TOKYO

> I DON'T THINK THAT WE ARE BORN WITH A FINITE NUMBER OF DREAMS. ONE THING ABOUT DREAMS IS THAT THEY CAN BE WHATEVER YOU WANT THEM TO BE, YOU DON'T HAVE TO PUT A LIMIT ON THEM, YOU DON'T EVEN HAVE TO KNOW THEM.
>
> — CHER —

Abbas had the honor of being flag bearer for the refugee team and had the flag affixed to his back.

As shocking as all of this was, none of it was really a surprise. Some things just are that way. You know they are coming but are still shocked when they come. I worked hard to focus on what a thrill of a lifetime it was for me to be here.

> *Even before the beginning of the trip, I knew that the Taliban was starting to take over. They were on their way to Kabul. After President of Afghanistan Ashraf Ghani told the army to surrender, the Taliban easily took over. I was hoping the Afghan army would fight back instead of running away. Ghani took off for Dubai, and the people followed what their leader did. Soon, the UAE and Pakistan, Iran, Saudi Arabia, and to a lesser extent, Germany, and the United States were flooded with Afghans.*

THE TRIP TO TOKYO AND A SPECIAL SURPRISE

Travel to Tokyo was so slow because of the global pandemic. Lines were long because we had to get tested for COVID-19 at each boarding. We traveled from Miami to Dallas with travel documents, green cards, passports, and special documentation. In Dallas they said that our notarized and hand-stamped documents were not good, and it took time to sort that out. Then, we had to get yet another COVID-19 test. The delays caused us to miss our flight to Japan, and we had to spend the night at the Dallas airport.

The next day, when we finally boarded a flight to Japan, American Airlines moved us into business class and blocked off part of the plane so that I could eat on the floor. My feet perform double duty as my hands so I need more room than other people in order to maneuver. The flight crew knew that I was part of the Paralympics and made it comfortable for me and Marty. They even took us off the plane separately from the other passengers. It was just the beginning of feeling very special.

The global pandemic elevated the pressure for both of us. We had to get special permission from the Japanese consulate to travel, and we had to stay COVID-19 negative.

Marty and I isolated ourselves for 30 days prior to leaving because we knew that if either of us were COVID-19 positive, we would not be going. Marty was also working every day as a masters swim coach while he was coaching me. He was overwhelmed.

On top of working and training and COVID-19, once the Paralympic team was announced, press obligations started, and to this day they continue. I was the only refugee with qualifying times for a medal. I never lost sight of what an honor it was to be here and I never forgot what it took for me to get here.

When we got to Tokyo, Negumi Aoyama from the United Nations High Commissioner for Refugees (UNHCR) greeted us at Narita International Airport and drove us for about an hour to the Olympic Village. I was falling asleep, and Marty was telling me not to sleep so that I could acclimate to the new time zone, 14 hours ahead. I remember how clean Tokyo was, and I saw beautiful shiny buildings, bridges, and rivers. I saw cars that I had never seen before.

From the minute we landed, we were followed by a Japanese documentary company who was doing a story about me. We knew that they were following us but they were not intrusive. This constant publicity was a necessary part of my life now.

Our room was fresh and comfortable and we slept great. Marty and I shared a room. We were already accustomed to being around each other all the time so Marty's snoring sounds did not bother or awaken me. In hindsight, I think that athletes should be together and coaches should be together. But for now, there were no other options:

After a good long sleep, we were called in to one of our first meetings with Megumi. She told me I was going to be the flag bearer leading the parade of nations for the opening ceremony. It was a total surprise and honor. I think that Marty was even more excited than I was. He kept telling me how this was an honor that would be with me forever and that this was so big. Now I was going to be more well-known, with even more attention on me.

Eight years after leaving Afghanistan, I led the parade of nations into the stadium at the Tokyo 2020 Paralympics opening ceremony.

The flag was very heavy. They had to strap a metal tube on my back and put the flag in it. It took a long time to fix the vest on me. They had to balance it and then I had to adjust walking so that I could wave the flag. Although this whole contraption hurt my back, I felt very strong that day. I was a leader. I was a lion. I was a king.

Here I was, eight years after leaving Afghanistan, leading the parade of nations into the stadium at the Paralympics opening ceremony.

The Paralympic flag bearer who led the parade of nations in the 2016 Rio de Janeiro Paralympics was my friend Ibrahim Al Hussein, a Muslim brother from Syria. He was in Tokyo competing again. His coach was 2004 Athens Olympian Alexander Tsoltos. Ibrahim and I became friends in 2017 after we first met in Mexico City at the Paralympic World Championship. Right now he is going through a lot. He has a lung problem, and I hope he is ok, and I include him in my prayers. It is difficult for us to stay in touch because our different languages make it hard for us to communicate.

There were some light moments in the seriousness of this competition too. In all the transportation to and from the pool, we had to wear masks. One time we made a picture for a missing swimmer and pulled down our masks then posted it on social media without masks on...I got in big trouble for that.

COACH ALEXANDER TSOLTOS

In the past it was Ibrahim's coach, who brokered the communication from Greek to English. Coach Alex explained it like this:"Ibrahim al-Hussein speaks Arabic and Greek. I speak Greek and English. Then I translate Greek to English for Abbas and English to Greek for Ibrahim. I was born in Greece but my mother is from London, which is how I know English. Just in case I cannot make it to the dinner table, Abbas and Ibrahim can say, 'I love you' and 'You are my friend' in each other's language.

"Both of them are Muslim Paralympic swimmers, who left their countries. Ibrahim is older, he was born in 1988; Abbas was born in 1997. They talk about their races, make fun of each other, and talk about their countries. Both of them have missing limbs. That is a lot to have in common. Ibrahim got disqualified during the breaststroke in the prelims and Abbas was there to laugh and take the sting out, that is the sort of relationship they have."

Abbas said, "We were making fun of Ibrahim running because he had to pee, so I made a joke about it. We used to make fun of a different coach who I had that used to eat too much and passed a lot of gas, so this was a continuation of that sort of humor. I met new athletes, too and it felt good to laugh with them. It was silly fun, and for these brief moments, my mind was not on what was happening in Afghanistan."

Coach Alex had this to say about Abbas: "I am amazed with Abbas. I saw him in 2017 in Mexico, 2019 in London, and now. I can tell in his warmup that he has matured as an athlete. He has the good fins that he needs to improve his kick, and good equipment, and he knows what he is doing. He is no longer an amateur. His progression is impressive, and he swims like a pro. His connection with Marty is apparent, and that has made a huge difference."

RETURNING TO FORT LAUDERDALE

We had 72 hours to leave Tokyo after the 50-meter backstroke. We didn't dwell on what happened. Megumi took us back to Narita International Airport for our flight to Chicago that would eventually connect to our flight back to Fort Lauderdale. We knew the airport processing could take from three to eight hours before we could board the plane.

We got yet another COVID-19 test and sort of recognized the area where I got my credentials. It took hours to get processed and more hours to get the special documents we needed. I did not recognize anything until I finally saw some artwork that looked familiar.

Unlike our flights on the way to Tokyo, we were simply passengers on a flight to Chicago, no one special. I did not get to sit on the floor so Marty fed me. During that flight I got stuck in the bathroom and needed help getting out of the small restroom because there was not enough room in there for my foot to open the door. In Chicago the wait was three more hours before our final flight left for Fort Lauderdale.

Both of us tried to calculate how long it would be until we could sleep. We wanted to be home.

I could finally relax enough to sleep without sleeping pills.

My family, all 15 of them, had safely crossed the border into Pakistan.

Meanwhile, when they got to the Pakistan border, my mom was trying to cross, and she fell. My brother had to quickly help her or people were going to trample her.

Megumi was able to help my family once they got to Pakistan. Because of my ongoing concern for their safety, I don't want to say in which city in Pakistan they are living. I felt so good that I was at least able to get her to help. My older brother Mohammadi has helped me so much in my life and took charge of the family during this crisis. He had many businesses in Kabul, construction, car sales, and building. He left it all to take our mother and the rest of the family somewhere safe.

> *The government of Pakistan is asking hotels across Islamabad to close reservations and place all rooms at government disposal for at least three weeks starting Friday to accommodate thousands of foreigners being urgently evacuated from Afghanistan.*
> *The directive comes in an official document from the office of the district magistrate, which was issued right after the deadly Kabul airport attacks.*
> *Even before the attack, scores of people were lined up on a major Afghanistan-Pakistan border crossing, trying to make their way into Pakistan.*

I later found out about all the other related things that were going on in the world...like this:

> *Delta Airlines pilot Alexander Kahn had a few days off from his regularly scheduled routes and signed up for an agent flight from Germany coded as a military operation.*
> *What he didn't know is that he would be flying a plane full of Afghan refugees escaping the violence and chaos to the U.S. for freedom.*
> *Several Delta crews met in New York's JFK airport to fly an empty plane to Frankfurt, Germany. "There was much chatter as we introduced ourselves and tried to figure out what the flights were all about," Kahn said.*
> *"We arrived in Germany on an empty plane. We figured out that this was an evacuation flight for Afghan refugees who left their lives behind and escaped Afghanistan without preparation."*

As he flew the plane with Afghans coming to the US, he said he was able to "put myself in their position."

"They're starting over. This is going to be a frightening experience for them but with huge potential."

Kahn understood. His own father was a Holocaust survivor who came to the United States with the clothes on his back, no family, no English skills, and had to start life over again, just like the passengers he was flying today.

I also learned what the United Nations High Commissioner for Refugees UNHCR was doing about the humanitarian crisis in Afghanistan. The UNHCR would later become an important part of my life.

The humanitarian crisis was escalating every day. These 3.5 million people lacked insulated shelters, warm clothes, fuel for heating, and enough food and medical supplies.

Temperatures were starting to plunge and many families lacked proper shelter, a necessity if they were to survive the impending cold.

After more than 40 years of conflict, Afghanistan remains one of the most complex humanitarian situations in the world.

Hunger in the country has reached truly unprecedented levels. Nearly 23 million people—that's 55 per cent of the population—are facing extreme levels of hunger, and nearly 9 million of them are at risk of famine.

Supplying food to help avoid widespread starvation is another immediate priority.

This year, UNHCR has assisted some 700,000 displaced people across the country since mid-August. The race is on to reach more. Right now they can reach about 60,000 people every week. Further resources are urgently needed for the most vulnerable, single mothers with no shelter or food for their children, older people who have been displaced and are left to take care of orphaned grandchildren, and those taking care of loved ones with special needs.

The UNHCR has been bringing in relief supplies by road through Afghanistan's neighboring countries and through humanitarian airlifts. Five more flights carrying UNHCR winter supplies from its global stockpiles in Amman, Jordan are scheduled next week.

UNHCR support will continue to help forcibly displaced families cope with the extreme conditions. The response includes core relief items, such as thermal blankets and warm winter clothing. Shelters are being repaired and reinforced, while others are getting plastic sheeting and insulation materials to help weather-proof their shelters.

Vulnerable families are also getting some cash assistance to meet additional needs during the coldest months, such as fuel for heating.

The UNHCR launched a global fundraising winter campaign to help ease the burden for forcibly displaced families amid the most life-threatening months of the year in Afghanistan and other countries across the world.

FOUR

BECOMING A UNITED STATES CITIZEN

> ONE DAY YOU WILL TELL YOUR STORY OF HOW YOU OVERCAME WHAT YOU WENT THROUGH, AND IT WILL BE SOMEONE ELSE'S SURVIVAL GUIDE.

The Immigration and Naturalization building near Fort Lauderdale, Florida.

I wasn't nervous for the citizenship test because I had already talked things out with God. I reminded him that he had tested me all I could be tested and that I had done my part to prepare and now it is up to him. If he wants me to be a US citizen then I will be a US citizen.

The United States Citizen and Immigration Services (USCIS) building is 20 minutes from where I live with Coach Marty in Fort Lauderdale. People driving past 4451 NW 31st Avenue in Oakland Park see a utilitarian yellow government building. Today it is the most beautiful place in the world because it holds the dreams of millions of refugees like me who want to come to the United States. This building is paradise.

During the swearing in, I wore the new blue suit that Marty got me at Macy's, and Marty wore a shirt with American flags on it.

When I took the citizenship test, we had to wait 25-minutes before a federal agent took us in. The USCIS is part of the Department of Homeland Security that oversees lawful immigration to the United States. Some of the services they provide include: Immigration of family members, working in the United States, humanitarian programs, and adoptions, I was glad the agent let Marty come in and sit next to me. It made me feel safe. I wanted everything to go perfectly; The Beast inside me was under control today. This was too important a day for any eruption. The agent looked Asian and wore a blue uniform with an embroidered Department of Homeland Security patch. He was very serious while asking me questions. Was I a terrorist? What is the biggest state? Was I in an organization? He checked my green card and travel documents and I signed a lot of documents with my foot. A lot of the questions on the citizenship test were things I had studied for. At the end, he gave me a slight smile.

On Friday April 1, 2022, I became a United States Citizen. This ten year journey was so hard. All the things I have gone through affected me but never destroyed me. I feel stronger than ever.

God and I both passed the United States citizenship test.

I had to swear that I would defend the constitution and abide by the laws of the United States. Marty and I were so happy. We went to Top Hat Deli not far from where we live and got big breakfasts to celebrate.

It is an honor for me to become an American and have an American passport. Now I can wear the American flag on my swim cap and train at the American Olympic Training center in Colorado Springs.

The Swim Fort Lauderdale team threw a big party and honored me with a cake decorated like an American flag and brought it out with lit sparklers. My friend Clyde Akbar played the violin and sang the "Star Spangled Banner" for me.

I was reminded that during these ten years as a refugee, I was never alone, I always had swimming and the wonderful people God put in my path.

INDIANAPOLIS: WINNING A GOLD MEDAL

Just a few days later, on April 7, 2022, I competed in the World Paralympic Games at the Indiana University Purdue University Indianapolis pool (IUPUI) where I won a gold medal, my first medal as an American. My time for the 50 fly was 36.36 and I also won a silver medal for my 50m backstroke. I don't like doing the backstroke because I come into the wall fast and hit my head. Swimmers with arms will come into the wall with their hand and touch it to determine the end. They can also more accurately judge the end of the lane by counting strokes from the flags. Swimmers without arms cannot do that so instead we get a clunk on the head.

THE DEDICATION OF RACES

I dedicated my races to my late father, Haji Nazir Hussain and my American Father Mike Ives. Both are gone now, and I will carry their legacy through my legacy.

I qualified for the 2022 Madeira Para Swimming World Championship in Portugal, and I have been selected by the USA Paralympics committee to represent the USA! This is my third world championship and my first one as an American.

Alhamdulillah. Thank God.

First, I need to train at the Olympic/Paralympic Training Center in Colorado Springs before going to Portugal.

THE OLYMPIC/PARALYMPIC TRAINING CENTER

I flew alone to Denver on United Airlines and took another flight to Colorado Springs where a shuttle picked me up to take me to the Olympic/Paralympic Training center. My room was like a nice hotel with a view of mountains and snow.

At first it was hard for me to breathe because of the elevation, something that takes a few weeks to get used to. I had to acclimate quickly because I was only going to be here for a couple of weeks.

The 50-meter pool there has the flags of all the countries, and right away I knew that this was a serious place to swim. Training is hard, two hours a day, and two times a week I did a double practice. We also did dryland training twice a week. The center is a first class, beautiful facility. I was here to train for the Paralympic World Championship in Portugal.

Because of the pandemic and because the new pools at the Fort Lauderdale Aquatic Center were not finished yet, I mostly swam in

25-meter pools. I am not yet officially on the main national team. If I win in Portugal, I get $7,200. To be on the USA national team, I have to drop my times. In the 50-meter butterfly, I am at 36.36 and I need to be at 33.32. It may take me a year to drop 4 seconds but if I do then I qualify.

I met my new teammates and coaches and everyone was so welcoming and nice. I had met most of them before I was an American citizen. They were expecting me, and I felt so good there. This is a training camp and the mentality here is all business. My new coach, Nathan Manley has been here a long time, and he has wanted to coach me for a while. I met him in 2016, and I have seen him in every competition. These people were not strangers. During my stay I had access to a physical therapist, a long course pool, and longer practices.

A nutritionist designed my personal food plan of delicious food. I had cupping on my back for the first time.

Cupping therapy is when a therapist puts special cups on your skin for a few minutes to create suction. People get it for many purposes, including to help with pain, inflammation, blood flow, relaxation and well-being, and as a type of deep-tissue massage.

Although its use is trendy now, cupping dates back to ancient Egyptian, Chinese, and Middle Eastern cultures. One of the oldest medical textbooks in the world, the Ebers Papyrus, describes how the ancient Egyptians used cupping therapy in 1550 B.C.

The cupping therapist puts a flammable substance such as alcohol, herbs, or paper in a cup and sets it on fire. As the fire goes out, they put the cup upside down on your skin for about three minutes.

As the air inside the cup cools, it creates a vacuum and causes your skin to rise and redden as your blood vessels expand. The suction feels so good and relaxing.

Every day I was there I would wake up and read email then go back to sleep. I would talk to my family and talk to Pari, an Afghan woman who I knew online. More about her later. Then I would go in the kitchen and eat fruit before stretching. I have known one of the other swimmers, Robert Griswold, since 2016, and he helped me put on my tight swimsuit, something I cannot do alone. Robert was a bronze medalist in Rio and a two time gold medalist in Tokyo. Robert has cerebral palsy that affects his coordination and strength. We ate together, talked about our lives, joked, and we went out and played in the snow. Robert and I have remained good friends, and I have the honor of being one of his groomsmen at his upcoming wedding in Colorado Springs.

If I win that $7,200 in Portugal, I will use some of it for a ticket to see my family again. I want to stay in Afghanistan for a while. I am in good shape physically, but mentally I am fucked up. I need to be with my people and see the girl who I only know from the Facebook messenger because she is an Afghan living in Pakistan. It was during this time that my family proposed to her for me and gave her a gold ring but soon that relationship became doomed.

For a few days, it was hard to believe that I was really at the United States Olympic/Paralympic training center, but reality set in when I started doing the work. It was very hard, and I had to be serious and focused. I fantasized about living in Colorado Springs. Like so many things I want to do, it all depends on money.

The training I got will be the same thing I will do when I get back to Fort Lauderdale. Marty knows the routine and also has some additional things for me to do. I have been having too much fun with our swim team in Fort Lauderdale. This is serious.

It really sank in. To be on the USA National Paralympic Team is a big deal.

PORTUGAL

To be a champion on this level, I have to always think about myself first. I must remain calm and control myself. No one will ever love me more than I love myself. I have been alone for ten years, and people really don't know what I have been through. I am so grateful for the people I have met along the way. So many times I thought I would not make it. It was often just too much to endure. Many times I thought that I would die and often I wanted to die, get hit by a car, a truck; just end it. I am not afraid to die. But while I am alive, I pretend to not need anyone but it is really just the opposite. I need others so much.

This was my first time in Portugal. I flew from Fort Lauderdale to Newark, and my flight was delayed because of a storm. I could hear the thunder. As a refugee I always had someone with me on airplanes but now I was doing it alone from Fort Lauderdale to Newark then joining the rest of the team from Newark to Lisbon.

Since I boarded late, I couldn't sit in the section of the plane with the other swimmers and eat my sandwich. I was so hungry so I sat with a Portuguese guy, and he helped feed me and give me Gatorade to drink. When I arrived in Lisbon, I got lost in the airport. I misplaced my backpack with my passport and had already left the secured area. I had not felt terror like this in a long time and was on the verge of crying. Security eventually found it.

I felt ridiculous and embarrassed. I simply got disoriented in the airport after using the bathroom and exited the terminal by mistake. I succeeded at being smuggled through Iran yet I somehow exited the airport terminal while the swimmers, the coaches and my backpack with my passport in it were at the gate. It was a shitty moment, and I got so angry at myself.

The meet in Portugal was the same Paralympic World Championship I swam in 2017 in Mexico City and 2019 in London. It was different this time because I had so much help. I felt safe and good about myself. All of this coaching and comfort and calmness helped me mentally.

What was amazing to me is how uncomplicated it is to travel with an American passport. As a refugee it was so opposite. First of all it is hard to get travel documents and you must wait for months for them. You have to get fingerprinted, another complication for me since I do not have fingers, and you have to have a recent picture. As a refugee, you cannot go to every country, not everyone will let you in. You get held up at both ends of any trip. Every year you must do this all over again. It is hard to get a visa. The reason I was successful at getting travel documents is because of my work I do for the UNHCR.

When I got to Madeira, I had my own room at the beautiful hotel, along with two caregivers, massage therapists, four swim coaches, and my own nutritionist from Poland who was very beautiful with green eyes. She would choose my food and bring it to me.

At the meet I swam the 50 fly and 50 back and lost by a fraction of a sceond, but I was so close. The final event was a mixed relay, and we broke the world record. We were the world champions.

The reason I even got to swim in the relay is because my roommate got COVID-19 and I was the alternate. Every day we got tested and every day I tested negative. I never got COVID-19. I have a world championship medal for the 200 relay, my best relay ever. It felt so good. Winning that gold medal was one of the best moments of my life, especially when they played the national anthem for me. I am so glad that swimmer Rudy Garcia Tolson whispered to me and reminded me to absorb this important moment.

The USA team members earn $1200 a month and now I have a good chance of being one of them. Although at this meet I was an alternate, they have a taste of me now. I felt confident that I would win.

In my beautiful hotel room were two beds, one for me and one for my gold medal. I swear I could have stayed there looking at it forever, but Coach Nathan Manley told me that I couldn't celebrate alone. I needed to be out there cheering for my team mates.

Look at me, first I was a refugee and the first refugee Paralympian. I proved to myself that I was good enough to be here at this moment. I worked so hard, and I did things my way, and it worked.

Before my 50 fly and my 200 medley relay I had a dream that I had won the relay.

A 200-meter medley is where four swimmers swim a 200-meter leg of butterfly, backstroke, breaststroke, and freestyle.

Then the dream came true.

THE OTHER THREE SWIMMERS IN THE RELAY

Elizabeth Marks: Backstroke

I have a special bond with another Paralympic swimmer, Elizabeth Marks. She lost her leg in the army while serving in Afghanistan fighting as a USA soldier and for Afghanistan's freedom. Ellie is fairly new to competitive swimming. Like all Paralympic athletes, Marks underwent an extensive classification process to evaluate her body's capabilities. Analyzers evaluate how her body moves in and out of the water, study her complete medical history and then label her on a number scale for each stroke. The physical scale is between one and 10—the lower the number, the more severe the disability. Doing it this way puts everyone on an equal playing field because you have such a variance of disabilities.

In breaststroke, Marks currently is classified at SB7, which means her lower body and muscles possess the same deficiencies as U.S. Paralympic National Team member Jessica Long, a double amputee, so they compete in the same group.

The system allows multiple people to hold records in the same event but for different classifications. Ellie swam backstroke in our relay. I swam butterfly. Since 2015, there had been no mixed relay because there was no butterfly swimmer. Because of me we could have this relay.

Rudy Garcia-Tolson: Breaststroke

Rudy became our breaststroker when my roommate Morgan Ray got COVID-19. Rudy was born with multiple birth defects, including Pterygium Syndrome, a club foot, webbed fingers and a cleft lip and palate...Garcia-Tolson endured 15 surgeries by the age of five before telling his parents he'd rather have a double leg amputation...By age 8, he had already become active in swimming, running and triathlons...At that age, he stated that he wanted to compete at the Paralympic Games and eight years later, he made good on his promise when he swam to gold at the Athens 2004 Paralympic Games. Since then, Garcia-Tolson has added more Paralympic medals to his collection including becoming the world's first double above-knee amputee to complete an Ironman triathlon in 2009...He has been featured on numerous media publications and television shows, including *The Oprah Winfrey Show, CNN, The New York Times, USA Today, Sports Illustrated* and was named as one of *People Magazine*'s "20 Teens Who Will Change the World"... Garcia-Tolson has won several awards, including the ESPN's ARETE Courage in Sports Award, Nike's Casey Martin Award, and was nominated for an ESPY...He continues to make an impact in his community through his work with the Challenged Athletes Foundation (CAF) and as a motivational speaker, sharing his message that "A brave heart is a powerful weapon."

Rudy Garcia-Tolson did not win any of his relays. He has five para medals and has not won anything since 2016. He has since retired and is now doing triathlons. This was his first relay since 2015.

Leanee Smith: Freestyle

She was diagnosed with a rare neurological muscle disease called dystonia in January 2012. She began swimming in 2013 as part of an aquatic rehabilitation session recommended by her physiotherapist. In August 2014, she encountered a setback when she began experiencing seizures and was hospitalized for two months. In 2017, as a resident athlete at the U.S. Olympic Training Center in Colorado Springs, Colorado, she set the American, Pan Am, and world record in the S4 50-meter butterfly at the 2017 U.S. Paralympic Swimming World Championships Trials.

Next year's Paralympic World Championship will be a tough challenge. Those Chinese guys who beat me in Tokyo will be there.

Being in Colorado Springs made me a much better swimmer, and now I have my teammates as my new friends.

After our relay broke the world record, and we got the gold medal, I got this email from Khaled Hosseini, the author of the Kite Runner and many other books. He is also from Kabul, and we are both part of the UNHCR. I admire him so much, and it means the world to me to have gotten this email from him.

Dear Abbas jan:
I am so happy for your win in Madeira. Congratulations! You are an inspiration to so many people. I will continue to root for you no matter what you pursue. Tabreek!
*** Best,***
*** Khaled***

When I returned to Fort Lauderdale, I stayed in celebration-mode for weeks. With the $7,200 I got for winning that gold medal, I planned my trip to Kabul.

Like always, I have been on the phone a lot with Coach Marty during the meet, he is such a constant in my life.

SIX
GROWING UP IN KABUL

When at a young age you learn to face fears, that makes the difference between people being champions and people not being champions.

Abbas' father shows Abbas to everyone by removing his shirt.

Just so you know, Afghans are not "Arabs" or "Middle Eastern." Afghanistan is not located in the Middle East. It is a South Central Asian country composed of many different ethnicities, none of which is Arab.

My father (my Atta in Dari), Hajji Nazir Hussain Karimi, had two wives before he met my mother (my Aaya in Dari), Golsam. Hajji means holy. Together they had nine children, I am number eight. Now my Aaya has so many grandchildren that I have lost count of how many, but I think it is around 15. Atta had two more wives after my mom. His last wife used to be married to my uncle (my Atta's brother) and when he died, my father married her.
Sharia law allows multiple wives for men.

I was born with a congenital limb deficiency. My arms didn't develop normally while I was growing inside my mother. The cause was never known. With congenital limb deficiencies like mine, the results vary widely from child to child, and researchers are still working toward understanding the causes.

Every year, roughly four of every 10,000 babies are born with an upper limb deficiency, while two in every 10,000 will be born with a lower limb deficiency. Some babies are born with both.

When I was first born and wrapped in a blanket, my grandmother came to see me. She loosened the blanket I was wrapped in and saw that I did not have arms. They did not know what to do with me, keep me at home or maybe take me somewhere else to be raised. My father committed to raising me the same way he was raising the rest of my 16 brothers and sisters. He asked our family to pour as much love and support into me as possible, and they did what he expected from them. My father took care of my grandfather, and he was going to take care of me too.

**ized*Dad told everyone to give me lots of love so that I should not feel lonely or alone. I didn't need pity, but I did need extra love because my life was going to be more difficult. He saw me as a test from God.*

My family knew that as a disabled Afghan, I would face stigma and discrimination with getting government services and being accepted. People like me are a low priority because Afghanistan has so many other problems that need more immediate attention. The United States has programs to help the disabled. Afghanistan does not. Everyone in Kabul is in a survival mode so there is a strict hierarchy of what is important.

After decades of war and conflict, uneasiness prevails during everyday activities and that is just the way things are. Kidnappings, explosions, suicide bombings, and threats are part of everyday life.

I learned at an early age to be fearless. If I have fear then I am done with this life.

My parents were riddled with anxiety and worry about how I would take care of myself and what kind of future I would face.

As a result, I got the most attention, the most love and the most care.

My father was the king of the family, and everyone was devoted to him and even a little afraid of him. People did what he said. His nickname was Dodge because he drove a Dodge truck. The powerful driver and this powerful car shared a name. He was also a well-respected leader in the mosque, something he later wanted for me too. He had a successful business selling cars and real estate, and all of us had comfortable lives growing up because of him.

While I was growing up, our family moved around to different areas in Kabul with each home becoming increasingly more comfortable. I remember Kabul's white sand and white dust and seeing a lot of government cars and soldiers with barking dogs. I was always bursting with energy, and I stayed outside a lot even though it was dangerous to do so. My strong will was a constant concern for my family.

A year after I was born on October 7, 2001, the US invaded Afghanistan to avenge the al-Qaida-orchestrated September 11 terrorist attacks. The primary aim of the US invasion was to hunt down Osama bin Laden and punish the Taliban for providing safe haven to al-Qaida leaders.

When the American-led invasion forced out the Taliban, Kabul was a forlorn place, much of it in ruins after more than two decades of Soviet occupation and civil war. By the following spring, it began to revive as more than a million refugees returned from abroad. Kabul's estimated population nearly doubled, to almost five million; the country grew from some twenty-one million citizens to forty million with the median age being 18.

In the nineties, the Taliban forced Afghans to conform to their stringent interpretation of Islam. Violators could have limbs amputated, or get publicly stoned to death. Women were made to wear all-concealing burqas and were prevented from holding jobs or attending school. Morality commissars hunted down graven images; in shops, men with markers blacked out illustrations on packages of baby soap. Even road-crossing signs for livestock were painted over. There was concern that this would all happen again. Safety was and still is, a constant issue.

Before that, Kabul was among the most beautiful cities in the world, with clean air free from pollution. It's surrounded by beautiful mountains that give the city a whitish look with the Kabul River flowing in its center. Before I was born, women could freely roam around the streets in dresses without being covered up.

I really was treated the same as all of the other kids in the family but they had to watch me closely and make sure that I was careful. My mother was always patient, kind, and a very devout Shiite Muslim. She kept our household organized and cooked great food for all of us.

Some of that attention towards me was simply taking care of my personal needs. Two people had to shower me, usually my sister and my mother. My mother wanted me to do well in school and be educated. She was always concerned about who would take care of me and how I was going to have a job, make money, and be independent.

When I would come home too late, she did not get mad at me, she was kind and simply let me be who I was.

All these years later, she still primarily wants to see me have a house, children, a wife, and afford a comfortable life no matter where I live. Of course she would love for me to live close by in Kabul, but she told me that if I stay in the United States and have a wife there then she is happy if I am happy. She knows how famous I have become. I always wanted to be something, and my drive was relentless. She is surprised at my success but at the same time she is not surprised. She let me blossom and create myself.

Now that I am an American, my passport allows me to go back there to visit anytime I want, maybe twice a year. My mother still always worries about me and will not be happy unless I am settled. I have that unsettled feeling too. No matter how hard I work, some part of me is missing. I need to go back there and see everyone with my own eyes.

I will need to get married soon, I am already 25 years-old and it is time. My family is always looking for someone for me. When I eventually do get married, I will leave my wife with my mother and brothers while I complete my goals in the United States. My heart tells me that this is the right thing to do and the right way to do it. The three brothers I am closest to are my biggest supporters.

MY FIRST LOVE, GOLSAM, MY MOTHER

My mother only wants me to be myself, she never tries to tell me to do something different from what I am doing. She is always hunting for the right wife for me. There are days when I miss my mother so much. I often cry about being apart from her, and she needs to see me too. She is getting older and has worked so hard at raising her own nine children, and now she is raising grandchildren. I have lost count of how many of them she has.

Mom is returning to Kabul from Pakistan with Mohammadi and she will be with my brother Alem and his family. It was hard to find enough work in Attock, Pakistan, a place many Afghans fled to when the Taliban took over. All of them will live with my brother Alem and his family in the house where I grew up. Asghar will also move back to Kabul. He was deported from Turkey so some of the family will be together again.

MOHAMMADI

I am 15 years older than Abbas, and I have been both a brother as well as a father figure in his life.

I knew that Abbas needed to leave Afghanistan when he was 16 years old. It was not safe, and I was worried for my own safety too. Afghanistan has different tribes, Pashtun, Tarjik, Hazara, and they don't like each other. The hate is very old and violent. Abbas was a swimmer with attention on him and that made it even more dangerous for him to be here. There was no future for Abbas in Kabul. He had to go. He needed to be independent and not have to beg for money or anything else. I prevented our father from making Abbas get married so young. He had important things to do. Abbas had the opportunity to become a Turkish citizen, and although that is far better than being in Afghanistan, his future was too big to settle for that option. It was not good enough for him to be in Turkey. I wanted to see Abbas in a place with more opportunity, a bigger country with the most support possible for his goals. Abbas had to learn to be alone and do things for himself. I know there is loneliness that comes with that, but he had to do it. He will suffer but he will learn too.

I have no regrets on the advice I have given Abbas. The paths I have chosen for him have always worked out. They were not perfect choices but the mistakes were learning opportunities for him.

I tell him now to never be arrogant, selfish, or cocky. Never forget your family and never lose your faith. Money is not that important, humanity is important, how you behave with others is important.

ASGHAR

My brother Asghar is three years younger than I am. He and I shared an upstairs bedroom when we were growing up. We slept on a mat and shared a big blanket that covered both of us. It was fun to have him there with me all the time. Asghar eventually went to live in Turkey where and met his girlfriend Eda there. We talk to each other often. The three of us speak Turkish, one of four languages that I speak, Dari, a dialect of Farsi, is our native language.

Asghar says:
I am really proud of Abbas. My head is high to have a brother like him. I tell the story about him all the time to inspire other people.

When we were kids, we played marbles, went to the river, and rode a bicycle together: I drove the bike, and he would ride on the back of it. We went to the mosque together, we swam together, and I was his bodyguard. We were friends with each other's friends.

We have never lost communication. Now that we are older we talk about girls and relationships, we talk about life goals and our respective sports, swimming and wrestling. We talk about what it takes to be a champion. We talk about our future.

I am a good wrestler and part of a wrestling club in Kabul. We have a trainer there too. We miss each other.

When Abbas recently visited Kabul, we stayed at the house where we grew up and stayed in the same room just like when we were kids.

ALEM

My brother Alem is a sales person. He is a devout Shiite Muslim and has a wife, three daughters, and four sons. He complains about his life in Kabul. He says he always feels in danger, and although he has enough food, it is still a hard life. He is a quiet soft-spoken man, and he and I talk about religion and faith. I hear Alem, I respect Alem but I do what I want. I never listen to anyone, it's not what I do. I control my own life and feel good about my decisions even if they are the wrong decisions.

Eventually my older brother Mohammadi took over my father's business, but when our family fled Kabul in August of 2021, my brother had to abandon that business and leave Afghanistan with whatever he could carry.

Like all the women, my mother wore a burqa when she left the house because Afghan women must cover themselves. When she went to Pakistan after August 2021, she was able to cover only her hair when she went outside, but when I was a child, she was totally covered with a screen in front of her eyes.

Our family was more fortunate than others. We had 16 kids (the additional kids are from my father's other wife) and three adults living there. I liked having all of those people around. My mother, my father, and my father's other wife were the adults, and nine of those children had the same mother as I did. The others are my step brothers and sisters. I respected my step brothers, but it was a distant relationship and we have not stayed in touch. I am number eight and the rest are older. I called my father's other wife "mom" too. She was always nice to me.

My brothers did not follow the tradition of having more than one wife. Sharia law allows Afghan men to take up to four wives with the understanding that a man must treat all of his wives equally although these regulations are rarely followed. To have multiple wives is a huge responsibility and expense. My father was up to it but my other family members are not.

The moms did the cooking and the housekeeping. Men do not do these things. We lived in a big house with a nice garden and a tall wall around it for protection. We had to go through a heavy metal door to get into our house. Protection and safety were very important and always there was an underlying tension and unsafe fear from the ongoing political conflicts.

Our garden had flowers, tomatoes, and other vegetables. We would eat that with the staple of the Afghan diet, Naan bread, a mostly flat and oblong in shape typically eaten warm when freshly removed from an earthen tandoori oven. A neighbor down the street from us had a tandoori oven and she made a little business out of charging the neighbors to use it. Women would make their dough at home and bring it for her to bake.

We ate the traditional cuisine of roasted meats or meat pies (*sanbūseh*), stewed vegetables, rice pilaf, and a thick noodle soup (*āsh*). We had fresh fruit and an assortment of yogurt-based sauces. I remember eating mangoes, peaches, and oranges with the doughy warm naan bread then falling asleep without eating dinner. To this day I still find comfort in doing that.

The moms seemed to like their roles at home and were devoted to my father. Their lives involved cooking, going to the market for food and necessities, and making our home comfortable. Our home was a welcoming place where we took care of each other. We always had the security of having enough money for what we needed.

I didn't really realize until I was around six years old that I was different from the other kids. My first memory of being respected for a physical skill was for playing marbles with my feet. The beautiful glass marbles made me happy, and I worked at making my feet flexible. I was so good at marbles, and people were impressed with what I could do. They would travel to see me play marbles, and I became a show, a form of entertainment and I got used to that kind of attention.

I began to collect the confidence to form my own identity and do things my own way.

I didn't look like the others and I didn't follow the others.

Thinking for myself often caused conflicts with the household rules. There were so many kids in my house that we had to have rules, but I just did what I wanted to do. The rules included things like, be home before it is dark, don't stay at other houses. I would keep my family worried because I didn't follow the rules even though I knew that my dad and Mohammadi would hit me. I was afraid of my father, but I still had to do what I wanted to do even though I paid the price. To punish me they would slap and hit me. That was the normal thing to do.

I understand hitting. Sometimes it is necessary if you need to punish someone; it is the right thing to do, and it feels good to hit. It is ok to hit girls too, but you must remember that they are not animals. I got wiser as I got older, and I don't hit anymore, but I still have the urge to do it. Anger makes me want to hit.

We didn't think of hitting women as beating or abuse. It was considered discipline and was rarely criminalized.
Women in Afghanistan are essentially invisible in public life, barred from going to school past sixth grade or working at most jobs. As in all war-torn societies, women suffer disproportionately. Afghanistan is still ranked the worst place in the world to be a woman. Despite Afghan government and international donor efforts since 2001 to educate girls, an estimated two-thirds of Afghan girls do not attend school. Eighty-seven percent of Afghan women are illiterate, while 70-80 percent face forced marriage, many before the age of 16.
Women who think about getting a divorce face this reality: she'd lose custody of her children and likely never marry again. Divorced women have custody of their children up until the age of 7, then children are given to their fathers.

I would rebel and break rules for the simplest things. If my family ate meals together I didn't always show up. Instead, I would buy ice cream and go to a movie house that showed movies from India with Farsi subtitles and watch a movie by myself. That was my favorite thing to do: I would drift into whatever world was in that movie. I still watch one movie a day. I have learned so much about cultures and language from movies. I would fantasize about being an actor in a movie and felt this special talent inside of me. I wanted to go to Hollywood and be in a movie, be in the fantasy.

I had little interest or passion for school except for learning English. To this day, I never really learned math and I still hate it.

However, I knew that I would need to know how to speak English. I was not happy in school and often did not go to school, although I loved going to the Shiite mosque with my family and other Hazara families. I knew all the other people there. I am a Shiite Muslim, and only 10 to 15% of Muslims identify as Shiite, the rest are Sunni. More than 85 percent of the world's 1.5 billion Muslims are Sunni. Shiites condense the five mandated prayers into three. They also keep their arms by their side in prayer, rather than the Sunni tradition to cross the arms.

My tribe, the Hazara people, are often killed when they are caught by the Taliban.

Hazara people are an ethnic group who are mostly from Afghanistan, primarily from the central regions known as Hazarajat. They established a large diaspora which consists of many communities in different countries around the world as part of the later Afghan diaspora. There are currently a million Hazara who live in the Balochistan province of Pakistan, mostly in Quetta, many of whom have been in the country for generations and are now Pakistani citizens. A similarly large Hazara community is also present in Mashhad, Iran, as part of the Hazara and Afghan diaspora.

Apart from Pakistan and Iran, many Hazara have migrated to Europe, and some to North America and Australia, mostly due to an unstable political and economic situation prevailing back home as well as the ongoing persecution of Hazara people in Afghanistan and Pakistan.

We would go to the mosque with my father on Fridays from 10 a.m. to noon and listen to the *ayatullah taqo desi* sermons from religious leaders and then pray. My father made me learn the prayers, and I did as I was told. What is amazing is that when I don't pray, God keeps forgiving me when I make mistakes.

Even today, I read the Koran. I do the five-minute morning prayer around 4 a.m., the 10-minute afternoon prayer around 1 p.m. and a 10-minute bedtime prayer. I bow and then I kneel. Before a swim race, I do a special prayer for strength.

These are the prayers that I grew up with. I keep the Koran next to my bed, and I read it one page at a time, the way my father taught me. He wanted me to be more religious like he was. I could talk to him about religion, and I remember how smart I thought he was even though he was able to read but not write. My father was a very religious person and highly regarded in the mosque. He taught me everything about my religion and I have a special connection between myself and God. In return, God has always put good people in my path. My father, brother, a woman I befriended in Turkey, the man who sponsored me to come to the United States, and my swim coach, Marty. I felt God through all of it.

My religion taught me to respect every single person and everything in this world. I don't judge the universe. I always seek hope in every single time of my life.

I brought the Koran with me from Turkey and I got another one in Portland.

I feel the strength inside from the Koran. My whole family soothes their souls with prayer and religion. I always liked religion and going to the mosque.

When a member of the community would die, funerals were at the mosque, then, all the people would eat together after. Everyone supported each other.

Religion makes me strong. I want to pray more, but I am so busy and so focused on my training. In my prayers, I pray for leaders who sacrificed themselves and suffered for Islam. I have learned to be at peace with God, and I know that God is looking out for me.

Growing up, our Shiite mosque held holiday services. The mosque holds about 200 people and everyone is on the floor rugs. Older people who are not flexible have younger people help them get up and down. It was always comforting to me that I knew all of the other families at the mosque. I still know most of those people and now we are Facebook friends. Most of the kids my age are now married with children. I found them all, and they know about me.

An example of a holiday I enjoyed was Ashura. We would celebrate it for ten days. The two main parts are fasting and

mourning. The voluntary day of fasting commemorates the day that Noah left the Ark and the day that Moses was saved from the Egyptians by God. There are mourning rituals and re-enactments of the martyrdom.

Shia men and women dress in black and parade through the streets slapping their chests and chanting.

Traditionally, Shia men seek to emulate the suffering of Hussein by flagellating themselves with chains or cutting their foreheads until blood streams from their bodies. Shia leaders and groups now discourage the bloodletting, saying it creates a backward and negative image of Shia Muslims. Leaders now encourage people to instead donate their blood instead of wasting it.

During the 10-day Ashura observation, we listened to sermons, drank tea and milk, and on the last day we had a rice lunch for everyone. I never skipped this. I liked being there with all the other people around. It was a solemn time but deeply meaningful, and I felt so close to God there. I can feel close without being in a mosque, but I'm closer with one.

WHEN GOD TAKES SOMETHING FROM YOU, HE GIVES YOU SOMETHING ELSE INSTEAD.

Outside of the mosque, I had boundless energy, and it was getting hard for my family to control me. I was out of hand. I didn't know then that they were trying to protect me. I just felt suffocated.

I knew it was dangerous for me to go out alone but I was fearless. I used to set fires and loved the orange flames and the danger of getting burned. I would jump over the fires, and this would attract attention to me. I used my disability this way to collect money to buy dried fruits so that I could share the fruits with my friends. I was learning how to leverage my disability to get what I wanted. As hard as my life was without arms, I was learning that there were things to take advantage of.

There was a special school nearby that was teaching English. I was not a student there but I knew people there, and often I had lunch at the school and could get someone there to feed me. All they needed to see was that I had no arms and I could just get what I wanted. Who would turn me down? It was a special school that taught English. I would play there, and I would also steal the toys from there and give them to my friends. The school was a 20-minute walk from my house. I liked to be there because the teachers were so pretty. Before the Taliban took over, women could show their faces.

As much as I enjoyed the attention I attracted and being a big shot at stealing toys and playing Santa Claus, frustration was mounting for me. I often thought about killing myself because managing my life without arms was just getting too hard. I had to always rely on others to do things for me. Plus, I was being called a cripple and getting made fun of by other kids. I felt a lot of rejection and judgment; people were calling me armless. I was a very angry kid. I was mad at the world and for my life not being fair. The worst part was that the other kids saw me as a person who was not capable of doing things. I questioned why God created me this way. Everyone else seemed to have an easier life.

I did have a few friends who saw beyond my disability, like Ahmadshah. He saw something special in me and told me that he knew I was going to be something someday. He would always tell me to focus on myself. He believed in me, and we are still friends. He lives in Chiba, Japan, where he is a car salesman. Because of the pandemic, I could not see him when I was in Tokyo. He always knew that I wanted to become a champion swimmer.

My frustration was mounting, and I got to a point where I didn't care if I lived or died, I just wanted to live my life my own way, and I resented everyone. My family knew that people were bullying me but they couldn't do anything. This was my battle. They encouraged me to go to school and learn whatever I could to make me independent.

Recently, I found a friend on Facebook that is living in India, but I don't want to say her name. She was in my English class. She said this about me: "Abbas was very intelligent, but none of our classmates knew that Abbas had his amazing talents. I remember the teacher asking Abbas to write something on the board. He went to the front of the class and wrote it with his feet. I was amazed how he did that and made it look easy. I was always proud of you, I was motivated by you, and I got energy from you. It was great to have you as a classmate. You dressed in a black coat and you were the smartest classmate."

BAND E AMIR

When I was very small, my family put me in the cold mineral-rich water in Band E Amir, a national park (now a UNESCO world heritage site) five driving-hours from Kabul.

This chain of six intensely blue lakes with natural travertine dams was believed to cure ailments. My father thought perhaps it would give me arms. At its deepest, the water is 150 meters and so blue.

Band E Amir didn't give me arms, but it gave me the magic to learn to swim.

My father knew my increasing discomfort. He had a photographer take pictures of me so that I could possibly get robotic arms. The problem with getting them is that I was growing fast so the arms would quickly be obsolete.

Now that I am grown, I could get robotic arms but I don't need them or want them. They add weight and are uncomfortable.

I was born this way and I cannot change the way I was created. I have made it work for me, and the universe must accept me for how I am. This is me.

Some people have everything and they are not happy. Some have mental problems. All these years of girls not liking me because I didn't have arms has made a full circle. Now, the girls like me this way. They find my drive, success, and perseverance attractive.

Confidence is more attractive than arms.

Since I did not go to school very much, I had time to explore other things. I played with dogs a lot and I developed the training skills to make them into fighters. With 40 years of war in Kabul, chaos is in their blood and in mine too.

I created new ways to use my situation and get people to pay attention to me.

I decided to become a beggar and found it was easy to get people to give me money. I would go to the nearby marketplace and hang around by the stores where I would buy dried fruit and Coca-Cola. I would go into a store and show them that I had no arms and they would give me money. It was so easy. Plus I got to be outside. The role of a beggar became just another performance arena for me.

I wanted to know what it was like to be a beggar. I didn't need to be a beggar, my father had money, but I did learn to understand a beggar's sense of hopelessness.

It was fun to ask strangers for money instead of asking my family. That made me feel independent. All these years later when I see beggars, I still give them money. Although I did not know how it felt to be poor, at many times in my life I did know how it felt to be hopeless. Beggars have lost their way. It is not their fault, and I feel relieved to give them money, even more so if they are disabled.

Even recently, while I was driving to an early morning swim practice, I saw a man with a white beard in a wheelchair. He had a dirty face and asked me for money. I gave him $10 and asked him to pray for me. For that moment, I felt what it was like to be a beggar again. Coach Marty is less trusting than I am, and he says many beggars are just scamming.

I often have to defend myself on the decisions I have made in my life, whether it is to give a beggar some money or to become an American citizen. I am in touch with many Afghans and they criticize me, saying that I have betrayed my country. I would be a piece of trash had I stayed in Kabul, so I had to do it this way. No one knows what life has been like for me.

A BARRAGE OF BULLYING WITH A DANGEROUS SOLUTION

When I was around 10 years old I sold drugs.

The oldest kid in our family was my brother Baqir. He and I have the same parents. Baqir hung out with people who did drugs, and he got addicted. He died when he was 33 years old and left behind his own children and wife. I have lost touch with them, but they know what I am doing. They live in Switzerland and came to see me in 2017 when I was in Geneva doing work for the United Nations High Commissioner for Refugees (UNHCR). They know that I became a US citizen.

I am not proud of the time I spent selling drugs. I delivered drugs for Baqir and made a lot of money for myself too. Looking back I still feel bad about doing this. I knew it was wrong but I was a fearless 10-year-old kid. I was also getting physically tough with my younger siblings if they did not listen to me. I would kick my younger brothers unless they listened to me. I was clearly headed for trouble.

I would have pockets full of cash from selling drugs, and I got to keep a lot of it. Baqir bought the drugs cheap and then sold them for a profit. Cigarettes, weed, hashish, and cocaine. He supported his family that way and he supported his own drug habit. Many Afghans support themselves through the drug trade.

Unlike Baqir, I never took any drugs, I just sold them. I knew it was wrong to do that but I did it anyway, I just knew not to get addicted. I saw what happened to people who did, and I thought drugs would kill me like they did my brother.

I excelled as a drug dealer because we knew no one would suspect that an armless skinny boy would do that. I would put the drugs in small bags then put those bags between my foot and the top of my sandals. It was a crime but not an enforced crime and just not that big of a deal. In Kabul, this is an available way to make money. There were always the traditional exports of carpets and rugs (which are nearly half of the total exports); and lesser exports like dried fruits and medicinal plants. Selling drugs here, however, was unprecedented anywhere else in the world.

MAKING MONEY IN AFGHANISTAN

With war, many sources of revenue were collapsing, forcing many of the farmers to grow opium for export.
Government officials regularly took bribes for turning a blind eye to drug trade. Mining of rubies, emeralds, tourmalines, and lapis lazuli, minerals, and precious stones is on a much smaller scale and much of it is done illegally. Crops are corn, rice, barley, wheat, vegetables, fruit, and nuts.

More than half of the people earn their money in farm related jobs.

Afghanistan is rich in resources like copper, gold, oil, natural gas, uranium, bauxite, coal, iron ore, rare earths, lithium, chromium, lead, zinc, gemstones, talc, sulfur, travertine, gypsum, and marble.

I was making $15 from each drug sale, an enormous amount of money to spend on food and movies. It was a shitty thing to do, but I did it for the money, then frivolously spent the money. I never saved any of it.

The whole drug problem solved itself because my family moved to another area so I could not deal drugs for my brother anymore.

When you don't go to school as a kid you have time to do other things. Besides begging, fires, skipping school, and dealing drugs, I had created my own life. It helped that I had the security of knowing my father had money for what I needed.

Besides the painful mental anguish and frustration I had just from taking care of myself, I was falling down a lot. I did not have the balance that having arms gives you. I would fall and get hurt. Around this time I was learning to do more things with my feet and learning to balance better. I spent my time playing soccer, practicing English, martial arts, taekwondo gymnastics and staying flexible. To this day I still practice the skills I learned during this time. I would cover my anger with fighting and kickboxing at around 12 years old, then channel it into swimming when I was around 13.

People say that sports keep you out of trouble. That was true for me.

In Kabul, we didn't have soccer or basketball teams or after-school clubs or even green spaces. We had kites and we made flying them into a competition. The goal was to sever the strings of other kites. Everything here is about fighting. I remember how the colorful kites would be back-dropped against the beige, dusty landscape. Handling the string would cut your hands and, for me, it cut my toes. The homemade string was made by a traditionally laborious process that involved coating cotton string with a concoction of crushed glass and glue.

Kite fighters speak of their craft as part science and part art. The key to excellence depends on a combination of factors, things you could see and things too great to be described in words: the flexibility and balance of the kites' bamboo frames, the strength of the glue binding the tissue-paper skin, the quality of the string, the evenness of the spool, and of course, the skill of the fliers and their ability to adjust to the unwelcome changes of the wind.

But factories in other more-developed kite-flying nations like Pakistan, India, Thailand, Malaysia and China now churn out tens of thousands of spools of machine-made nylon fighting string that swamp the Afghan market. Unlike in other Asian countries, like Pakistan and India, where kite-flying is wildly popular, Afghanistan's kite industry is still homespun and humble. There is still no Afghan kite federation, no national competitions, no marketing. While nearly all the string sold in Afghanistan is now factory-made and imported from other countries, lots of the kites are still made by local artisans.

There is a block-long market of tiny kite shops in Kabul, the Shor Bazaar.

Seeing the kites is a reminder of beauty amidst the chaotic debris, the smoke from a suicide bomb, the relentless traffic. When I was young I loved to fly kites even though the strings would cut my toes. My brother Mohammadi was really good at it. Women were never allowed to fly kites, and eventually the Taliban forbade kite flying for everyone.

This Afghan kite culture was the backdrop for the bestselling novel *The Kite Runner*. The author, Khaled Hosseini, became my friend through our mutual positions with the UNHCR. Khaled also has his own foundation and interviewed me for his foundation and we have kept in touch. I have autographed copies of Khaled's books with personal messages, and he regularly congratulates me on my swimming victories. Although we have only spoken on zoom, at some point we are going to meet in person.

I was headed for big trouble and I knew it.

By this time I was drowning in my own anger. I was always getting into fights with bullies who would mock me for my disability. I skipped school, played marbles, went to the river, ate whatever I wanted to, and was mad at the world for making my life hard. I could feel the rage building inside of me.

My brother Mohammadi and I talked about my future. How was I going to be independent? What was next for me? I was tired of being in Kabul. I was not listening to anyone. My family was telling me to study, go to school, and stop fighting. I was getting punished for hitting people with my head and feet. My nose was often bleeding from getting punched and kicked in the face. I didn't even care if I won the fight. I didn't care if I got punished. I still have some of those scars on my body today. A rage kept building inside of me.

The one place that provided tranquility.

One of the places we lived was See Bangi, close to the Kabul River and a recreation area.

I found solace playing in the river. The water cooled me off, calmed me down. I liked watching the sun shining in it, the feel of it, the sound of it, the color of it, I was attracted to all of it. Mohammadi worried about my being safe in the water and initially discouraged me from going in the river. It was another place where people would judge me when they saw me in the water with no arms.

I learned that the world sees us disabled people differently. We must show our capability and talents. Our hearts are not disabled. Everyone is going to doubt us, and I have been faced with this my whole life. Even my family doubted me. I needed more independence. I needed to not need them.

My friends and I would go into the Kabul River with our clothes on in an area that was not so deep. When we got out of the water the warm sun would dry our clothes. I became a swimmer in my mind then. I loved everything about the water, how it felt on my skin. It soothed me and I went there whenever I could.

One time the current of the river took me to where there was fighting and I got scared. The fighting was scary. I heard guns but mostly I quieted down in the water.

SWIMMING

My brother Mohammadi was part of the construction team that built Lajward Water Complex, the largest indoor swimming pool in Kabul in 2012.

Construction took eight months to build and cost about $600,000.

It was a half-hour walk from our house and became a popular place for Afghans who could afford the 500 rupiah ($10) entrance, a hefty price in a country where the average yearly income was $585.

Lajward Water Complex was built by an Iranian man who grew up in Kabul and wanted a place for young men to go. Qasim Hamidi, trained as an athlete and worked as a swimming coach in Iran, Turkey and Uzbekistan. He was also the director of Afghanistan's water polo federation.

Hamidi returned to Afghanistan to promote swimming and said this pool would make it possible to train properly. He said that many Afghans want to exercise but there aren't many places to do so. With a pool like this, there would be opportunities to win competitions and show promise for a future Afghanistan.

MY FIRST SWIM COACH: QASIM HAMIDI

When the pool first opened I came to see it and visit my brother Mohammadi who worked construction there. I went there every chance I could to be near the fresh still water. It was so much calmer than the river. I was terrified to go in the water over my head because I thought I would drown.

Qasim saw how much I loved the water, and he encouraged me to take off the bright orange life vest I would wear; so I tried it. I was scared to do it at first but my confidence grew.

Little by little I learned to swim. At first I learned the backstroke then how to use my legs for breaststroke and I came there every day to do it. Qasim got in the water and locked his hands behind his back and showed me that it was possible to swim without arms and that I should try to do it. It took me a week to totally acclimate. I also learned to get in and out of the water by myself.

Qasim taught me a couple techniques and I started thrusting myself in the water to propel myself. I showed Mohammadi what I could do and then other people there saw me. I already loved the feeling of the water. I found it interesting to learn this. We didn't care about technique, it was about getting comfortable. I kept returning for more and more, and Qasim recognized the drive in me. This was a new kind of independence for me. When I was in the pool, I didn't feel different from anyone else. I was so happy in the water. Soon, I could actually swim on my back. Just six months after—at age 13, I started competing. I created my own workout plan too. My family came to swim meets and were so proud of me.

Qasim said to me, "I'm going to make a hero out of you. I am going to make you a champion." He knew that if I learned to swim that I would become something.

Qasim got the local television station to do a story about me. He is the one who brought the public to the pool to see what I could do. He knew I wanted this. Without Qasim, who I consider my very first coach, I would never have started swimming, and he is part of why I am now a champion. He had a lot to do with it.

By this time he and I started talking about the Brazil Paralympics in 2016, and Qasim was speaking to the Afghanistan Olympic Committee about holding a slot for me. I had four years to train and bring a medal to my country.

Qasim said, "I have trained swimmers for 20 years, but I never saw anyone like Abbas, initially so scared, so curious and so relentlessly driven."

The pool was open from 8 a.m. to midnight, and because I also got a job working at the pool, I was able to swim there. Qasim was there every day too. My brother, Asghar, and I worked in the store where they sold hair oil and shampoo. There was a steam room there, a jacuzzi, a cold plunge pool, and a cafe that served hamburgers, sandwiches, and pomegranate juice. If you didn't know better, this pool could have been anywhere in the world, except there were no women there. Women are not allowed to swim.

I worked at Lajward for two years. That job gave me a place to swim, provided some money, and kept me out of trouble.

People would come from all over to see me swim and encourage me and say that I was amazing. I would wear a t-shirt to swim because I did not want to show myself. Soon I was swimming two hours at a time.

By this time I had taught myself to eat, drink, turn on the shower, and write using only my feet. I was growing more confident and independent. If I could not swim, I would have focused on taekwondo or kickboxing or Thai martial arts Muay Thai. I would have done that, and I would have been a champion at one of those things. It was in me to be a champion.

Qasim also taught me about social media, how to post things, what to post, which sites to use, and how to promote myself. He likes to say that he did everything for me, but ultimately, I was the one who did it. His help was monumental and I will always be deeply grateful to him.

It was not always easy for Qasim to run Lajward. Electricity was available only three days a week, and even when it was on, it was not consistent enough to run the pool filters or heat the facility. He had to rely on a generator, and some days the cost of doing this would be more than any profits he made on that day.

There was also some local opposition. While the pool was being built, some officials demanded bribes, and others complained about it not being proper to have such a facility in the neighborhood.

I never gave up on swimming. If I did, I would never have progressed. I wanted to learn and grow every day. That is how you get what you want.

GETTING TO KNOW 'THE BEAST'

WATER DOES NOT RESIST. WATER FLOWS. WHEN YOU PLUNGE YOUR HAND INTO IT, ALL YOU FEEL IS A CARESS. WATER IS NOT A SOLID WALL, IT WILL

NOT STOP YOU. BUT WATER ALWAYS GOES WHERE IT WANTS TO GO, AND NOTHING IN THE END CAN STAND AGAINST IT. WATER IS PATIENT. DRIPPING WATER WEARS AWAY A STONE. REMEMBER THAT. REMEMBER YOU ARE HALF WATER. IF YOU CAN'T GO THROUGH AN OBSTACLE, GO AROUND IT. WATER DOES.

— MARGARET ATWOOD —
(FROM *THE PENELOPIAD*)

By this time, a rage and anger built up inside me like a volcano. This Beast inside of me has become both my best friend and my worst enemy.

The Beast is the monster that will explode like it did at the Tokyo Paralympics after the 50-meter butterfly finals. That was an example many people saw but it was not the first time I have felt like the transformative Incredible Hulk.

The Beast had its beginnings when I was a little kid. I noticed that when someone called me armless or cripple, or told me I was small, a rage would overcome me. Those names meant to me that they thought that I was useless, and the thought of being useless was scary to me. Part of this is my own doing because I reach for lofty things and that puts an enormous stress on me.

I think that if the goals that I continually set were more reasonable, more people would have them. I reach for the extraordinary.

When the Beast surfaces within me, all rational thinking disappears, and predictably, trouble for me ensues after. As a kid, I would fight and kick and hurt people with wild abandon because it's The Beast who is in control, not Abbas. The Beast hurts people who are close to me and also hurts me, and I don't feel any remorse…at least at first. My chin, above my upper lip, my forehead, my nose all have scars from the years of The Beast fighting.

The Beast also talks rudely to people I love. Be forewarned: when The Beast emerges, stay out of his shit. Leave him alone. I regret it when The Beast overpowers me but The Beast is bigger than me and has his own path. After The Beast has an outburst, I feel terrible about what I have said and done. It has happened with Mike, the man who helped bring me to the United States from Turkey, and with Marty, my dedicated Paralympic swim coach. These men are my American fathers; they are irreplaceable; they are everything to me. Yet, The Beast still takes over sometimes.

Sometimes The Beast enters just to give me a way to unload stress and listen to myself.

I get angry at the world. Now that I am a world champion and an American citizen, everyone is nice to me. Where were all of you when I needed you? Sometimes I get angry about that and that will trigger a visit from The Beast. This rage makes me disrespect myself and everyone else.

When The Beast is present, he never cares if he hurts someone but is filled with remorse later and sincerely apologizes. It is as if The Beast is a wild animal who lacks any human part.

Sometimes waking up The Beast is predictable like, when someone is trying to control me. I am the leader, and no one tells me what to do. The Beast is so mean. I hurt people, destroy them, and love them all at the same time.

The Beast within me has done terrible things. I actually told Mike Ives, the man who brought me here from Turkey, I don't need you, just kick me out and stay away from me.

He would look at my food and simply ask what it was and The Beast would insult him. The Beast has gotten angry at Marty during the swimming warm up when he gives me water. There is no reason or excuse for any of this. I know that it is wrong and it will ruin me if it keeps happening and I am working on controlling The Beast. If I don't control The Beast, eventually my only companion will be myself.

My internal rage comes from being alone for so long. I get mad at God for making my life hard and making me function with a handicap. I question God and often ask him why he let my father die before I could see him. My father did not get a chance to see what I became and that makes me angry. When I get angry about that, it will trigger a visit from The Beast.

The Beast, however, has a good part. The Beast has helped me figure out my life. The Beast will never let me give up on myself and is my best friend in the world. When I am serious, he is my confidant, my protective best friend, and my leader.

The Beast emerges at key times in my life like when people did not think I could be anyone or was not good enough. He has shown his teeth to the women who have rejected me and has a growl or two if people see themselves as better than I am.

There isn't a lane mate or gym partner or running buddy who is better to have with me than The Beast. Maybe God works in tandem with The Beast in his plan for me. I focus on the good, and it has gotten me this far so—cut me a little slack. I am an injured horse, and my emotions are tired.

BEGINNINGS OF DEALING WITH THE MEDIA

I got used to the media early on. They were always around me when I competed in swimming. It is because of the media that people know me, and I always felt that journalists were my supporters. The media has helped me all through my swimming journey. My first contacts were through Al Jazeera, the Arabic-language cable television news network that has been compared to CNN. It is a mix of news, talk shows, educational programs as well as a forum for uncensored news and editorial freedom, unique in the Middle East. It was founded in 1996 and is transmitted from Doha, Qatar. Since 1999 Al Jazeera has had continuous programming.

Never try to imitate anyone else.
Follow your own path, find something new,
something that is yours, and stick with it.

— *Ricco Gross* —

*German biathlete and the only biathlete
in history to win four Winter Olympic relay titles*

Abbas at the $370 million Tokyo Aquatics Centre.

People trying to leave Kabul, at Hamid Karzai Airport.

This Gift

The 2021 Refugee Paralympic Team.

Opening ceremony; Abbas carrying the Refugee Flag.

Tokyo Paralympic team with Marty and Teddy (back row).

Megumi Aoyama from the United Nations High Commissioner for Refugees

The bedroom at the Olympic Village. Abbas got to keep the quilt.

Ibrahim Al Hussein lost his lower right leg during the 2012 Syrian war. His father initially encouraged him to swim.

Alex Kahn.

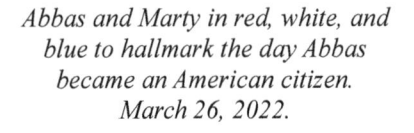

Abbas and Marty in red, white, and blue to hallmark the day Abbas became an American citizen. March 26, 2022.

Swim club teammate Clyde Akbar singing the Star Spangled Banner and playing the violin.

Cake to celebrate Abbas' passing the citizenship test and Marty's birthday.

This Gift

The gold medal relay team.

At the Team U.S.A. Olympic & Parlympic Training Center in Colorado Springs.

U.S.A. Paralympic Team.

Elizabeth Marks hugging Abbas after winning the Gold Medal.

Gold medal in the World Paralympic Swimming Chapionship in Portugal.

Elizabeth Marks and Abbas.

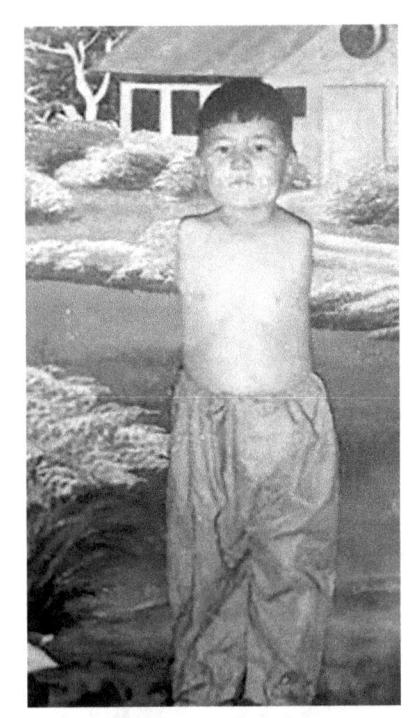

Abbas as a little boy.

Childhood in Kabul.

Abbas's father.

Abbas's medals with his father's hat.

Abbas at his father's grave.

Mohammadi and Abbas.

Band E Amir, A UNESCO World Heritage Site.

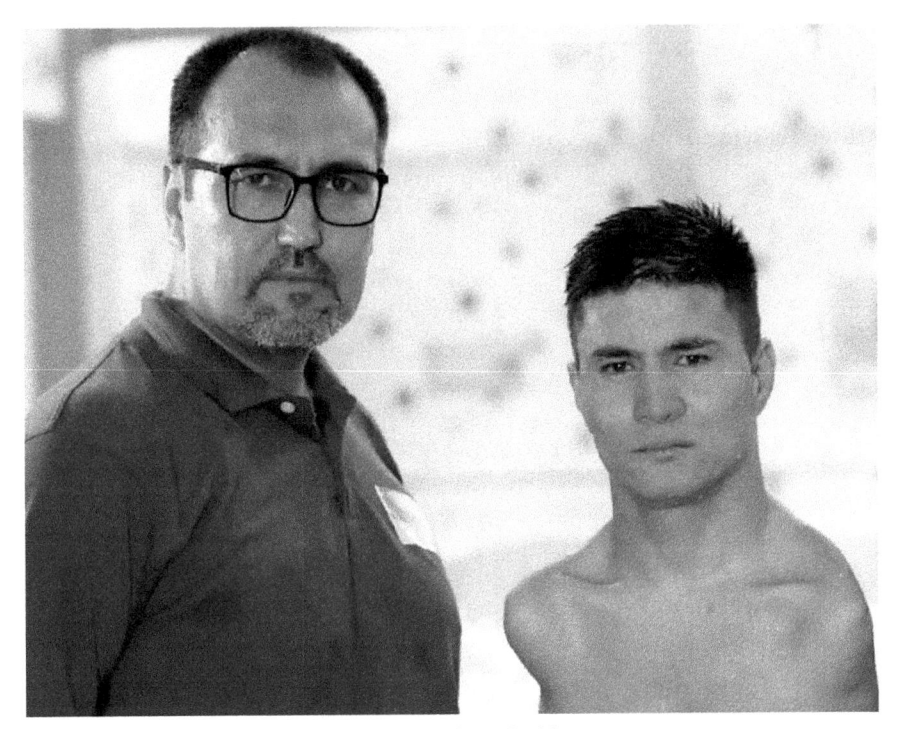

Qasim Hamidi and Abbas.

Swimming awards in Kabul.

Abbas at the Lajward Water Complex.

Makeshift gravesites in Iran of the refugees who did not make it.

This Gift

Abbas and Senem Yagci in Turkey.

President Erdogan invited Abbas to become a Turkish citizen.

The UNHCR members on World Refugee Day.

Claire Lewis, the UNHCR Global Goodwill Ambassador Programme.

*The **Time 100** interview with Angelina Jolie.*

Multnomah Falls, near Portland.

Norman Santos, Mike Ives, and Abbas.

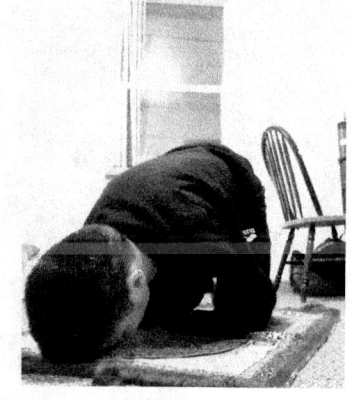

Abbas praying with his prayer mat.

Oregon Reign Masters coaches.

Brother and sister, Allen and Linda Larson.

Chehalem Fitness Center, Oregon.

Abbas and Coach Allen Larson.

101

Texting with his feet.

Thumb's up!

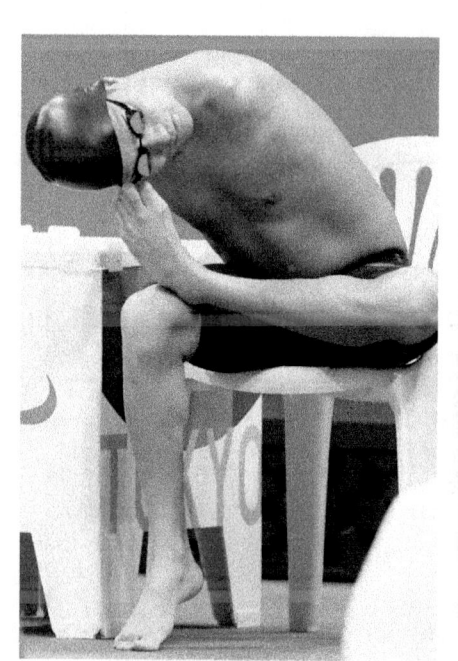

Abbas scratching his ear.

Driving the red Ford Explorer.

Swimmer Magazine article.

Marty, Abbas, and Coach Chris McPherson

Swimming with dolphins.

Abbas and Marty at the Golden Goggles awards.

Abbas and Alex Blavatnik from USA Swimming at the Golden Goggles Awards.

Abbas and Mark Pinger from Arena Swimwear at the Golden Goggles Awards.

Abbas at a celebration dinner.

Abbas and Mike Ives.

Mike with several of the people he helped.

Abbas at Carter Park in Ft. Lauderdale, Florida.

Marty coaching.    *Abbas in Mexico City.*

The Ft. Lauderdale City Council declared July 20th "Abbas Karimi Day."

Abbas and his brother Hussein in Miami.

The International Swimming Hall of Fame (ISHOF) diving well in Ft. Lauderdale, Florida, under construction.

The Fort Lauderdale Aquatic Center, home to the International Swimming Hall of Fame.

Abbas speaking at the American Advertising Federation's Choose954 meeting.

Abbas' family.

At the finish line.

DON'T FEAR FAILURE.

LOW AIM IS THE CRIME. IN GREAT ATTEMPTS, IT IS GLORIOUS EVEN TO FAIL.

— BRUCE LEE —

SEVEN

HATCHING THE PLAN TO LEAVE AFGHANISTAN

> When a man has an appointment with grandeur, he dares not stop at comfort.
> — Tennessee Williams —

Map of the journey and the Middle East.

The Lajward hosted Afghanistan's first-ever disabled swimming competition. A local television station was there, my father and my brothers were there, and I won the competition. We had eight swimmers and we swam four at a time. My goggles fell off my eyes and were in my mouth during the race. With no arms, I could not put them back on so I had to finish the race this way.

I did my 25-meter breaststroke, then my 25-meter backstroke. This was the first para meet ever in Afghanistan. The prize for the winner was 10,000 rupiah which is around $200 but the money never came through. That was typical of how things are done here. That was a turning point for me. If I wanted to be anything in swimming, I had to leave Afghanistan. It wasn't the money, it was the knowledge that there was no future for me as a swimmer here.

For the first time, I could clearly see my whole future in front of me. It was getting more difficult for my mother and sister to give me a shower now that I was maturing and it was awkward. My father thought that it was time for me to get a wife. That way she could take care of me and eventually my children could. The wife might be someone a little older, a leftover girl. I wanted a virgin girl, a beautiful girl. They were concerned that no one was going to marry me. How would I work? How would I support a wife? I had one thing I was good at, swimming. I wanted to stay away from my family because they didn't think that I would be ok. They were wrong about me. It felt like they did not believe in me so I just wanted to be alone in my own world. I wanted to be a champion, make history, go to the Paralympic Games, and be rich and famous. I knew that if I stayed in Kabul I would have the wife and kids and be in the mosque. I wanted to be special and that was never going to happen here. To my family, I had everything in Kabul. To me, I knew I could have that and much more.

Mohammadi encouraged me to seek my dream and leave Kabul. Yes, I had a loving family, but I had no future. I was so happy that Mohammadi believed in me and helped me figure out how I was going to do it and gave me the money to make it happen. When I was ready to go, I told my family that I was going to Iran to figure things out, and I kissed my father's hand. He thought I might stay in Iran for a while and become a mosque leader and find a wife. Mohammadi knew that he was disobeying my father by helping me with the plan. Safety was an issue. Iranians are Muslim but are different from us. My family prayed for me and gave me money.

What I was going to do was illegal. I was a scared 16-year-old with a visual disability and that was a lot for me to carry. My mother cried and encouraged me. She knew there was not much for me in Kabul and that I needed to go and pursue the dream that I wasn't going to find here. My father did not cry, and I did not cry. I was excited about the new journey.

The tears came later and often.

THE FIRST THING WE DID WAS FLY FROM KABUL TO TEHRAN.

My brother planned the trip. Mohammadi and I took a two hour flight to Tehran. Mohammadi had a round trip ticket, but mine was only for one way.

I took a backpack with a few of my clothes, the Koran, my prayer rug, my USB portable flash drive with my swimming videos, my martial arts video, video of me eating and drinking using my feet and driving a car using my feet. I needed the video to show what I could do and use it to get help getting into another country. I thought it would be a lot easier to get help if I showed that I was independent and had a special skill. For the next four years, these would be my only possessions.

I still have that USB flash drive, and I want to add to it and have someone do a professional job reformatting it.

We stayed with my brother's friends for a week. I tried to get some help from the United Nations in Tehran, but since I was not an Iranian citizen, they could not help me, and I couldn't go back to Kabul so I had to proceed. Mohammadi arranged for me to be illegally smuggled across the Zagros Mountains to the Turkish border.

The Turkey-Iran border.

"Go to Turkey," Mohammadi said with confidence, "they will accept you there." Mohammadi had to return to Kabul because of work and his own family.

During our time in Tehran he and I went to mosques and holy places. Mohammadi insisted we go to the place where they were putting dead bodies in coffins, and he made me look at that. He told me that no matter how good I am, no matter how many things I do right I could still end up here. That is how the world is. Ten years after that day, and for the rest of my life, I will never forget that.

People stared at me in Tehran too. No matter where I am, people still look at me the same way when they notice I don't have arms. I see it in their eyes.

The journey from Kabul to Turkey was whatever the opposite of smooth, comfortable, and safe is.

I cried when I left Mohammadi and went with the smugglers. They sent a younger boy to help me, and when he said goodbye to his own family, it made me sad all over again. That boy, Ahmad Rahimi, stayed in Turkey, eventually went to Europe, and now lives in Sweden. We still communicate once a year or so although the whole time we were together we fought and argued. He had a cocky way about him and took pleasure in teasing me. The Beast beat him up too.

Mohammadi paid the smugglers $750 up front and gave me the other $750 for me to pay them when I reached Turkey. Teams of people coordinate the smuggling and no one crew takes you the whole way. There is a mountain crew, a road crew, and in part of the mountains we walk ourselves. The smugglers provided horses for the rugged terrain in the Zagros Mountains and some of the other people rode on them. For $50 you could ride a horse, which was too expensive for me. I only had $200 separate from the smuggling fee.

My phone was the only way to contact the smugglers. It is still hard to talk about this. When I revisit that time in my life I get anxious all over again. About 30 people were making the trip with me and we were all in the same truck. We became supporters of each other. The first road was dirt, and the truck was shaking the whole time. We would go for a while and stop. Then another truck picked us up. They covered us with blue plastic so that no one could see us. On the way to the Turkish border more people would get in. Five big Pakistani men got in on top of us. They couldn't see me because I was covered and they piled on top of me. It was getting hard to breathe because we were all so close. All of our feet touched. When we got to the first mountain range in, we had to walk until another truck came to get us. The path seemed never-ending and it started to get really cold. This mountain range covers much of southeastern Turkey and roughly follows the western Iranian border. There are pistachios, almonds, grapes, pomegranates, plums, apricots, wild barley and lentils growing here. It is very beautiful here and that was a sharp contrast to the misery I was feeling. We saw lots of people doing the same thing we were, but rarely did we ever see people going the other way. I did hear about two Persian people who decided to stay in Iran. I understand that a journey like this is not for everyone.

About 20 wild dogs tried to attack us but we scared them off by throwing sticks at them. We had to spend the nights in the mountains to avoid the Iranian police. It was September and still warm and I didn't anticipate the coldness as the elevations increased. I also didn't bring warm clothes, no heavy jacket, and I had only sports shoes so when they got wet, my feet were very cold. I just focused on the belief that if I got to Turkey then I would be ok. The journey took three days. My biggest fear was being caught by the border police. In their custody, they could kill me, rape me, or simply deport me back to Afghanistan. I heard the stories.

The days were endless. I could not speak to my family or anyone I knew. I had to save my cell phone battery for later. There was no cellphone reception in the Zagros Mountains. This mountain range is full of deformed crystal rocks that extend for over 1500 km from eastern Turkey in the northwest through to the Gulf of Oman in the southeast. It was exhausting to walk and difficult for me to balance on those jagged rocks.

I read the Koran and prayed to God a lot. At night I put my head between my knees and tried to stay warm. In the mornings my legs were totally numb. I could not feel my legs and could not walk.

I had to move forward no matter what. I had never been so cold in my whole life. I already accepted the reality that if I died, then I died, but there was no going backwards. It was too late to change my mind.

I regretted doing this. It was not worth it, and I wished I had stayed in Kabul. I would have my family. I would have my mom, my dad. If I had to do this journey with arms it would still be impossible, but I had the added handicap. There were no choices for me. I had to do it. I was out there alone.

This was a horrible, scary journey.

I was not sure that I was going to survive this trip, and many people did not. I would have just been one of them. I prayed that I wouldn't get caught being smuggled. My focus was only this: If I could just get to the Turkish border, I would be ok.

The mountains were beautiful, and I remember one of the smugglers had a beautiful daughter. I just kept walking on the jagged rocks.

My caregiver and I argued about everything. He made me uneasy and taunted me. I wanted some of the fresh bread that he had and he would not give it to me. Then he would laugh at me and shove that bread in my mouth, almost choking me with it. I got mad at him and hit him in the head. I did not want to break his bones or make him bleed. I just wanted him to feel some pain. I had hate for him and we were not friends.

All of us who were being smuggled had this in common; we were fleeing difficult circumstances, and we knew this journey across the hostile Zagros Mountain crossing was not going to be easy. Our group had Afghans, Pakistanis, Syrians, and Iranians. This area of the Iran-Turkey border had become an important route for migrants moving westward. Some made it, others died along the way—that is just the way it was.

GETTING TO TURKISH BORDER

The border crossings have concrete walls and barbed wire barriers but that does not stop the mostly young people from fleeing despair, conflict, and violence in search of a better life.

None of us who were doing this had prospects for a decent future at home so we had to leap into this unknown and gamble on the dream that, for many, turns out to be a nightmare.

When we reached the obscure part of the Turkish border, the wall was about four feet high, and I needed help getting over it. This area looked almost deserted. We all climbed over and started cheering and hugging each other on the Turkish side. Then we went to the smuggler's house, and he gave us more food. I could not eat the very salty cheese. We learned that some other people had spent a month walking across Iran.

We had successfully dodged the border police. I got over the wall, I felt warm again, my stomach was full, and I was in Turkey. My new life was about to begin. I would be able to train without the fear that I had in Kabul.

Many people who were with me planned to find a job in Ankara, Turkey, send the money home, then eventually move to mainland Europe.

We were kept in a safe house for a few days. Many people found shelter under bridges, in abandoned barns, or they slept out in the open. Others traveled in groups of five or even ten. Often they had to split up with a telephone as their only communication.

For the survivors who have made it this far, the next stop is usually Diyarbakir, the largest city in southeastern Turkey and the honorary capital of the Kurds. There, migrants and refugees wait for days for someone to take them in a bus. In the meantime, they live off the charity and goodwill of the locals.

Most of them will have to make it on their own beyond this point, once they realize they have been abandoned by smugglers who have stopped picking up their phones. Although the smugglers were doing something illegal, they were decent enough people who were just making a living, and they were then on to smuggling the next group.

The first town in Turkey is Van. Some people came here with smugglers like we did. Others come by buses or enter on foot through a winding road, but few people remain here. Their goal is to keep moving west where there are more opportunities. Human trafficking is barely concealed here. Buses often crash after the snow melts in the spring. This is when the villagers find the bodies of the asylum seekers who died somewhere along the way. Their graves are marked by slabs that say *Afghan* or *Pakistan,* or just simply the date they died…mere traces of their lives.

Only Mohammadi and I knew the plan. When my father found out I was not coming back to Kabul, he was shocked. He got angry at Mohammadi for helping me, but years later he forgave him for doing the right thing for me. I wasn't sure at this point where I wanted to go from Turkey. I had a brother in Melbourne, Australia, but he wasn't a citizen there; I had cousins in Sweeden, and Italy was another place where many Afghans went. I was open to living in many places.

I realized much later on, after my father died, that living at home with him was the best thing ever. I would give up everything to see him again. I miss him so much, and I see him in my dreams. He just wanted me to be taken care of. I know that I have become a person he would be proud of. Swimming helps with my sadness and that suffering is part of the big dream. High risk and danger are part of it too. I suffer a lot and I am angry about that. Why does this all have to be so hard?

EIGHT
LIFE IN TURKEY

*If you have a big enough why,
you figure out how.*

— Logotherapy —

I will either find a way or make one.

— Hannibal —

During the Second Punic War, 218 BCE

My brother, Asghar, who eventually arrived in Izmir City, Turkey.

I was worried about my younger brother Asghar. He didn't understand where I had gone. We were together all the time, we always slept together. He was only 12 years old and he missed me. I missed him too. Years later, he came to Turkey after I had already left there. He has a Turkish girlfriend, he speaks Turkish now, and the three of us talk in Turkish on Facebook Messenger.

The girls in Turkey dress like the Afghan and Iranian girls but they do not cover their heads, and I kept staring at their beautiful shiny hair. They also wore dresses with no pants and I could see their legs. I felt so guilty about how much I liked seeing them. I knew it was wrong but I liked it. I was overwhelmed by how pretty they were and I was getting constant erections. Girls here have so much freedom. Many Muslim women choose to wear the headscarf as an expression of their faith and cultural identity but they have the choice to do so. Women in Afghanistan have no choice, they must begin to cover themselves when they are 10 years old.

The first time I spoke to my family was when I got to Turkey where I could finally get cellphone reception and find a place to charge the phone battery. Once I got to Turkey, I had to be careful about how much I used the phone; in 2013 cell phone minutes were expensive.

The smugglers took us to a house one night in Van and cooked us an omelet and even made extra for us to eat on the bus. While the bus was being checked out by local police, I was folded up in the luggage compartment because the bus driver wanted to protect me. It was so dark in there. Because of my flexibility and because I have no arms, I can fold up to be very small. I was scared when I saw the police but they were nice even though I was there illegally. I was just one of the people in Van doing the same thing as everyone else.

My mother had some distant relatives in Malatya and I stayed with them for a while. It was fine at first, but there were too many people in their house, plus there were three teenage girls there and I was getting too excited around them. It was sad for me to leave some semblance of family, but this was just a stop to regroup on my journey.

I took a bus to the United Nations High Commissioner for Refugees (UNHCR) in Ankara and registered with them to get help. Although the Turkish government runs the refugee camps, the UNHCR looks for vulnerable people to help and I wanted to be included. There are over two million refugees in Turkey and I was fortunate to have a place to go now. I was sent to an orphan camp in Kastamonu with other refugees, the first of four refugee camps I lived in.

CAMP 1

I unpacked my backpack with my prayer rug, my copy of the Koran, my USB video storage stick with video of me swimming, driving, and feeding myself, along with a few clothes. Those were my worldly possessions. The orphan camp was close to Kastomanu and it was a shelter for kids under 18, most of whom were Turkish, but there were some asylum seekers like me. I showed my United

Nations papers there and this became my home. I practiced maneuvering my body so that I could shower and dress myself. Every day I did stretches that I learned in kickboxing to keep my body flexible and balanced. People don't realize how much arms keep you balanced. I had to compensate for my unsteadiness by practicing balance.

There were 50 or 60 of us at the camp. Four of us shared one room and we had a television and a computer. They forced us to go to school where I had to wear a uniform of a jacket, pants, and a tie. After school I got to swim and some days I got to swim in the morning too. We were fed five times a day, mostly soup, chicken, rice, and some bread. At this point I was getting better at showering myself but not proficient yet. My feet have to act as my hands and as flexible as I am, I cannot reach enough yet to get fully clean. The beds were hard and lumpy but I was grateful to have somewhere to sleep. Two women cleaned our room, and it was our responsibility to keep it neat.

We had neither air conditioning nor heat; temperature control amounted to opening a window or closing it.

There were strict rules about minors leaving the camp on their own. I kept telling people at the camp that I was a serious swimmer and begged them to find me a place to swim. They arranged a meeting with a coach and access to a 25-meter pool. I started going twice a week, and I entered a local swim meet where I won the 50-meter freestyle event.

There were some good swimmers in that competition and I was glad that I could swim there. First I went there twice a week, then three times, and then I asked for four times. The people at the camp grew weary of my persistence.

This was the first time I ever saw girls swimming; they are not allowed to do so in Afghanistan. Women in Turkey wore skimpy tight body-hugging suits like in the US and they were so sexy. I went crazy when I saw them swimming. This was all so new to me.

The pool was near the camp. Kastamonu is a nice city with 12th century Byzantine castles, historic mosques, and dense forests. It also has the Ilgaz National Park where people ski and mountain climb. This area was part of an 11th century trunk route to the Euphrates River. It was beautiful there and famous for the last total solar eclipse of the millennium that occurred here in the towns of Cide and Gideros on August 11, 1999.

I could have stayed there for a long time but I was having problems at the refugee camp with the other kids. Once again, people called me cripple and armless, and once again, The Beast in me surfaced and started fighting with the other kids there. We would make up after and be friends for a while, but my tolerance for them was weak.

My temper grew more out of control and I was getting into fights all the time. One of the kids told me that I couldn't use the computer, and he pushed me. I got a big cut above my lip and was bleeding. Who was he to tell me what I could and could not do? When I challenged him he would not fight me face to face. The police even came to the refugee camp. The Beast wanted to punish him for this. He slept in the same room where I was sleeping, and The Beast even thought about killing him by hitting him very hard, but I knew not to do that. I let it all go. I forgave him, and soon after I left that camp.

Everyone but me had responsibilities at the camp since there was not much I could do without having arms. Other people resented me for what seemed to them like a privilege. They also resented my getting special permission to swim.

I had a great three months of swimming there but I had to leave because they could not take care of me anymore. The Beast was emerging often and I was combative and getting in physical fights over use of the computer. I kicked and injured a Turkish boy during soccer.

I was aggressive and I was angry. I was angry at God for making my life so hard and angry at myself for losing control. When I go outside, people look at me strangely all the time. It was so hard for me to do everything, I was falling down and hurting my head. I couldn't balance. When people made fun of me, The Beast would come out. I was facing another glitch: I was getting sent to another camp.

My plan was to take all of that aggression and channel it into swimming.

It was time for me to leave my assistant Ahmad and for him to make his own journey. For the entire trip from Tehran, he and I constantly fought, but when Ahmad left me he cried and cried. I was confused. We did not like each other. I did not cry. Maybe he was crying for himself and it had nothing to do with me. It was hard for me to understand this. Crying comes to me at unpredictable times. I didn't cry when I left my family but I cry at other things. Maybe his crying was some sort of displaced emotion too.

CAMP 2

I got to the second camp in the middle of the night. This was a rehabilitation camp for people with disabilities and was about two hours by car from Istanbul.

Some people at this camp had more than one disability. There were disabled kids in wheelchairs who played basketball. There was a guy there who was deaf, blind, and could not speak. I made friends with Errol, a blind guy. Errol thought that I should be in a place that had swimming only, as if something like that existed. He and I were together all the time and we always ate together. We would talk about girls. I kept asking to be taken to a swimming pool. Finally they took me to a pool an hour away and sent a caregiver for me because I cannot put on and take off a swimsuit or goggles. The swim coach there was impressed with my swimming and said that he could make a champion out of me. I had goggles and fins but they were not in the best shape.

I was on a bus for an hour to get to the pool, then back an hour to have lunch, then an hour to get there again, and an hour

to get home. I did this twice-a-day commute for 8 months. I did a double practice every day and was so exhausted that I slept on the bus. Day and night I was hungry to swim and train, and I tolerated the discomfort because I wanted to be a champion

By this time I was crying a lot, especially before I went to bed. Many times I regretted leaving my home, and I wanted to go back to Afghanistan. At the same time, my swimming got faster. I went to the Turkish National Championship and got a gold in the 50-meter butterfly, a gold in the 100 backstroke, and a bronze and silver in other events. I was the only refugee from a camp who was in the swim meet; everyone else was Turkish.

People saw me swim and said, "Who is this guy? He is not Turkish." I got a lot of offers from a lot of teams who wanted to train me and make me a Turkish citizen. I went back to my camp as a hero after this championship.

Swim meets in Turkey are serious because the swimmers are being selected for the national team, something I could not be on because I was a refugee, not a Turkish citizen.

I sheltered myself from others by swimming. By now my Turkish was getting better, and I even learned a few bad words. I already spoke Dari, Farsi, and English, pretty good for a kid who never went past 9th grade.

I was 16 years old and I was worried about myself. I was homesick, and I cried a lot alone because my family was so far from me. Ten years later, it is not all that different. I am still homesick and I still cry alone; it is just that now my surroundings are more comfortable. Swimming and the gym make me feel less alone, and I have to remind myself that I will do great things with what I have. I must always remember why I made the choice to leave Kabul and how far I have come since making that choice.

CAMP 3

This camp was a rehabilitation camp for people with disabilities. I was the only person there who was not Turkish. I stayed at the third camp for eight months and became close friends with a Turkish nurse there, Senem Yagci.

She was married and had a son around my age, and we were friends. I helped her son swim, and I played soccer with him. I encouraged him. Senem gave me a lot of his nice clothes and brought me chocolate. Mostly she gave me lots of love. I was so needy, and I needed her. She gave me money too. It was too hard for her to take someone home who was in a wheelchair, but it was easy for her to take me. Her husband seemed like a nice man but I didn't get to know him. Senem had a house with an upstairs, and they had an extra room for me where I would go on the weekends. She cooked for me and fed me and was there for me. I used the internet there and Skyped with my family. I also was starting to post videos on Facebook of myself swimming then answering people from all over the world who saw the post. My family met Senem on the phone, and my mom told her how much she appreciated her looking after me. Senem was one of the people who helped me. She took me to the movies, she took me to see things in Turkey, and she treated me like her own child. She was so proud of me when I won the Turkish national championship. We still keep in contact even now. I have moved on from so many people in my life, but it was very hard for me to move on from Senem.

I was getting scared of the life ahead of me. Other than Senem, I had no close people, not much money, no country, and no passport. I could not compete internationally because of this. I did a reality check and really questioned if I was going to make it.

I was willing to go to a lot of different countries. It was all a risk. I also had the opportunity to stay in Turkey and become a Turkish citizen. They wanted me, the coaches wanted to train me, and to this day, when I see Turkish swimmers who I knew from then, they say they are sorry that they lost me. The competitions were in Istanbul, about an hour from the camp. The coach would pick me up at the camp and take me back.

I thought about becoming a Turkish citizen and it was available to me. Turkey is not as free as it is in the United States. I would not be able to drive a car, the opportunities for me are more limited, but the opportunities for me are better than in Afghanistan. Maybe this was good enough. There were a lot of pluses in staying here. I already spoke decent Turkish, I could swim here and I was wanted here. It was my brother Mohammadi who convinced me not to stay in Turkey. He thought I could do better, and once again, he helped me make this tough decision. I was asked to leave this camp eventually because they could not take care of me. Now I was beating up disabled people and making people cry. I can be very mean, it is part of The Beast. People at the camp didn't care that I was winning swimming events, they resented me because of the special privileges I got because of swimming. I was just too problematic and I had to leave.

The third camp was a rehabilitation camp 90 minutes from Istanbul, and it had younger people than the second camp and more disabled people. I found a swim team and a coach, although I could tell that the coach really didn't care about me other than I could help him make a name for himself. I have that kind of insight. I was a displaced person with a refugee identification, so that limited me. I could not compete outside of Turkey.

> *I can tell when people don't care about me, and that coach didn't. I recognize opportunists.*

The coach tried to convince me to become a Turkish citizen. He had government connections and thought I could benefit Turkey. What is amazing to me is, later on, when I was chosen to come to the United States, he said that he made that happen. He was only interested in himself.

My best shot at getting closer to my goal was to reach out again to the UNHCR. I had the information about how to contact them and learned how slow their processing was. In the meantime, I kept posting my videos on the internet showing what I could do, how I swam, how I drove a car, how I fed myself. The video not only showed my skills, I showed my independence this way. I was posting something at least once a week and got a lot of Facebook followers. People would wish me success and offered many compliments and comments, but there were no offers for me.

HOPE

One of the people who followed me was a man from Portland, Oregon who saw my videos and encouraged me to come to the United States. Mike Ives said he was a retired teacher and was looking for someone to help and that he had helped many disabled athletes before.

As beaten down as I was, as defeated as I felt, the communication with him gave me hope. Maybe he was a scammer or some sort of human trafficker, but he offered to help me, and I believed him. He started paying for my internet so that we could talk more. The camp gave me some money, and the Turkish government also gave me some money. My internet signal was weak, that is when it was working at all, but I hung on to this bright spot.

I told my family about Mike and like always they were supportive of me. I spoke to them once a week, and sometimes I spoke to Qasim too, mostly on Facebook Messenger but to keep the costs down we limited talking to once a week. I let them know what was going on in my life. As much as my family missed me, they never asked me to come home.

Mike and I worked on the UNHCR together, and he would not let them forget about my case. His relentlessness encouraged me. I felt like I had a partner who was smart and seemed to know what he was doing. Mike said that he had already helped other disabled athletes from Colombia, Philippines, Thailand, Mexico, Iran, Vietnam—all of them with high potential.

Meanwhile, the UNHCR was looking to possibly send me to Australia since my brother Hussain lives in Melbourne, and having family is a placement consideration. The people working on my case were Persian and Turkish. They also knew that Mike wanted to sponsor me in the United States and that I could live in his house in Portland, Oregon. The UNHCR knew what I had to offer a country. I was a high-level disabled swimmer and I spoke English. We never let this possibility of coming to Portland go and both Mike and I kept contacting the UNHCR.

Many times I just wanted to give up and admit that nothing was going to work and that really it was better for me to be in Kabul with my family and figure out another way to do this. The UNHCR people were warm, nice people, and they told me to be patient and not to give up, but I often got frustrated.

By this time I was getting more independent. I kept learning to take care of myself by practicing things over and over until I could do it. I learned to wash my hair with my foot and religiously stretched to remain flexible enough to continue to do so. I asked for help sometimes but preferred to do things myself whenever I could. I still felt discouraged but I believed in God, I believed in swimming, I believed in Mike and in my family, and I also knew that Turkey wanted me to become a citizen. All of those things were encouraging, but I was still lonely and sad.

Other people in the third camp noticed that I got special attention. They saw that I was creating a way out for myself and they resented it. I had national recognition for swimming and they were jealous of it. I trained twice a day, every day, and I won 15 medals including two Turkish national championships—and I wasn't even Turkish.

I was even honored and photographed with Turkey's President Recep Tayyip Erdogan and offered citizenship in Turkey. They took me to some sort of formal tribunal, and when the judges asked me if I wanted to represent Turkey and swim for them, I told them no.

I carefully considered the offer but I knew that I had a limited future in Turkey. My brother Mohammadi told me not to do it and to wait for a better opportunity. I trusted him. He has a good sense of these things. People say I should have accepted the offer and that I made a mistake by leaving Turkey, but I don't regret it. Yes, they were right about this part: I missed a lot of swimming opportunities, international meets, and the Paralympic championships that would have been all during my prime swimming years, with age 21 as the prime year. Because I had no passport and no documentation, I could not compete in these international meets.

Even with national recognition, swimming medals, and the glimmer of a better future, my anger often overwhelmed me, and I had to leave the third refugee camp because of fighting. I was getting into fights with other people in the camp and physically hurting them. The fights were always about the same issues, asking people to do things for me, people making fun of my disability. I was told that this camp could no longer take care of me and I was sent to a fourth camp close to Istanbul

CAMP 4

The fourth camp was in the outskirts of Istanbul and near a pool. It was also the worst of all the camps. It was dirty and overcrowded, with refugee kids from everywhere, Somalia, Africa. Instead of four people in a room, there were ten of us in one room. Because of swimming, I had some freedom to come and go. I could swim nearby but not every day. I kept my master plan pretty much a secret. I did a lot of dryland training, kept to myself, and just focused on my goal. People wanted to train with me and I was respected for my skills. That motivated me even more to be a champion.

My typical day at camp number four was like this: I would sleep wearing headphones which would transport me into my own world. I slept great because of this because the music would soothe me. Sometimes it was too loud and woke the others.

When I woke up, I would do my morning prayer then go running, usually a 5k run. When I came back, I would have breakfast, rest, and get ready to swim. I would do a lot of stretching and practice martial arts. After that I would eat again. The food at all the camps was consistent, rice, soup, chicken, and some bread.

I was totally focused on myself. I still had some distant admiration for girls but no girls were living or working at the camp so it was easy to detach from the idea of them. Girls were a distraction I did not want.

I didn't form any lasting relationships at this camp, and I found most of these people not worthy of keeping in touch with. Once I asked someone there to bring my bag, and they thought that I was being bossy and demanding by asking them to do things for me. When I wore a big jacket, I got accused of hiding my arms. I pretty much kept to myself. I told a few people what my plans were but not many. I had very few possessions but I had accumulated more swimsuits, fins, goggles, and caps that were given to me.

By this time I was chatting with Mike Ives every day. He later told me that while I was in Turkey, he had some doubts about me really being able to swim. He was leery about me as I was leery about him. He admitted that he really had no idea how to bring me to the United States, and he was learning how while doing it.

Mike was spending hours of his time helping me and asking his church, his congressman, and other politicians for help and advice. I learned later how much he invested in me, a person he never met and that he worked on it constantly for two years.

Of course it was ridiculous how much faith I had put in a stranger, but Mike was all I had. At first I thought he was crazy. I was totally ignoring the 11-hour time difference between us and calling him while he was asleep.

No matter what time it was, he would always talk to me.

Back then my English was not as good as it is now but I clearly understood this: I had no future if I stayed at the camp and that coming to the United States would be a new beginning for me.

Mike and I were communicating daily now, and I trusted him more and let go of the doubt I had about him. He cared about me and we liked each other. Still, people were telling me to beware of him, that he had ulterior motives, that he would somehow use me. I knew that Mike was supporting other refugee athletes right now. I knew that he was a former wrestling coach and a retired special education teacher. Initially he had wanted to help an armless kid from the Philippines. The kid was a fisherman and he had to catch fish to eat. That kid died, and Mike was devastated that he could not help him.

I used the money he sent me for the internet, for shoes, and things I needed.

Mike gave me what I needed most at this time of my life. Hope. I had hope.
I believed in Mike Ives.
Some of the other kids at the camp were jealous of the attention I was getting, but I knew it was more than that. They were jealous that I was creating a way out.

With all this promise for my future, I still felt the reality of being alone and the possibility that none of this would ever work. I often thought about just giving up. Maybe it was better for me to just give up and be one of those people who was walking back home through Iran while everyone else was walking the other way to freedom. Maybe there was a better way. I also knew that the UNHCR would never support me if I did that. As a refugee, I did not have a country. When you don't have a country, you don't have a nationality. You can't enroll in school, see a doctor, get a job, open a bank account, buy a house, or get married. Millions of refugees are without a nationality. I could not return to Kabul. At night I would put my headphones on, lie on my bed quietly, and cry.

I was calling the UNHCR whenever I could and so did Mike Ives. He wanted me to come live with him. I am grateful for the Turkish government. They kept me safe, they fed me, and when it was my time to go, they released me. I was a resident there and had a refugee identification, but I was not a citizen.

Often when someone is resettled, they have to learn the language and get trained in a skill. I already have both. My disability makes me a priority. I speak English and am an accomplished athlete. I also have someone who wants to sponsor me and a place to go. That makes me a good prospect for integrating with the country.
Of the millions of refugees, these things put me in the one percent of refugees who get resettled in the United States and that is why I never gave up.

My advice for refugees is if you have to leave your country, know what you want to do and don't ever give up. It is a huge risk and life will be hard.
Your goal will be what keeps you going.

NINE

THE UNITED NATIONS HIGH COMMISSIONER FOR REFUGEES

>   Say what you would be
>   then do what you need to do.
>   — Epictetus —

The office of the United Nations High Commissioner for Refugees (UNHCR) was created in 1950, during the aftermath of the Second World War, to help millions of Europeans who had fled or lost their homes. They had three years to complete the work and then disband. UNHCR now has more than 18,879 personnel working in 137 countries. The budget, which in its first year was US$300,000, grew to US$8.6 billion in 2019.

The year 2020, marked the 70th anniversary, and during that lifetime, the UNHCR has helped well over 50 million refugees to successfully restart their lives.

Today, over 70 years later, the organization is still protecting and assisting refugees around the world.

The UNHCR goodwill ambassadors are celebrity representatives of the Office of the United Nations High Commissioner for Refugees (UNHCR) who use their talent and fame to advocate for refugees. These Goodwill Ambassadors and Messengers of Peace are distinguished individuals, carefully selected from the fields of art, literature, sports, science and entertainment,

To be assigned as a UNHCR Goodwill Ambassador is an official postnominal honorific title of authority, legal status, and job description assigned to those goodwill ambassadors and advocates who are designated by the United Nations. These people represent sports or other fields of public life and have agreed to help focus worldwide attention on the work of the United Nations. Backed by the highest honor bestowed by the Secretary-General on a global citizen, these prominent personalities volunteer their time, talent, and passion to raise awareness of United Nations efforts to improve the lives of billions of people everywhere. My goal is to become one of these UNHCR ambassadors.

The same relentlessness I have through swimming helped here too. I was calling the UNHCR every day to process my case and, Mike Ives was also calling and sending them emails. I never met the people in person who were working on my case, but I eventually met other people from the UNHCR. They were warm, caring people who explained to me that the process of resettlement takes a long time and asked me to be patient. They also emphasized that my being available for their calls was important.

During the next two years I had multiple interviews and cultural orientation discussions. The Turkish government said my situation was very specific and everything was customized to fit. I never missed a scheduled meeting with them.

Resettlement programs vary from country to country. In the United States, UNHCR works closely with U.S. governmental agencies and non-governmental organizations (NGO's) who are responsible for resettling refugees in the United States. An NGO includes charities, churches, community-based organizations, lobby groups and professional associations.

Information goes from the UNHCR to these partners and the general public about refugees around the world who need resettlement.

The United States has the largest resettlement program with five basic steps.

Here is how it was for me:

1. First, they investigated my personal information and background. They wanted to know if I owned a gun and if I knew how to use it. Was I in a terrorist group? They also wanted to know about my family. I also had an interview with someone from Homeland Security and Citizen and Immigration Services. Then I got my own case file.
2. I had an interview to see if I was eligible to come to the United States. It is called the Refugee Status Determination Interview. This is where it is determined if I am considered a refugee under international law.
3. The process takes nearly two years and includes more medical checks and interviews.
4. When the screenings are finished, travel arrangements to the United States are made, and all the travel visas must be secured.
5. I was getting resettled in Portland, Oregon. Travel costs are paid for by the United States, and they provide temporary cash, medical assistance, and case management to help with the transition to become self-sufficient.

My visa from the UNHCR showed that I was a refugee and that the United States accepted me. This allowed me to cross borders. I had no criminal background, I don't do shitty things, I was a swimmer and a minister of hope for myself and for other people.

I am so grateful for what they did for me, and I am devoted now to helping other refugees like I was helped. I don't know where I would be without the UNHRC. I started off as a youth advisor for the UNHRC and am on track to become an ambassador. Right now I am a high-profile supporter.

Through speaking to groups about sports, I help motivate and encourage refugees. My purpose in doing this is to use my notoriety to bring attention to the plight of refugees and to advocate for them.

WHO ARE THE CURRENT GOODWILL AMBASSADORS FOR THE UNHCR?

The UNHCR helps people who need to flee their country and seek asylum elsewhere. They won't be sent back to the country that threatens their life or freedom because of race, religion, nationality, political opinion, or membership in a social group. This is considered a rule of customary international law.

CLAIRE LEWIS
UNHCR Global Goodwill Ambassador Programme

I met Abbas mid-2015 and got to know him as a refugee. He became part of our youth advisory and we immediately had a good rapport. He was training to be one of six athletes on the refugee Tokyo Paralympic team. Before we met him, he already had a lot of impressive wins.

Abbas is a natural leader and has the ability to inspire. Angelina Jolie was our special envoy at that time and she interviewed Abbas for us.

He spoke for the other athletes and was very skilled at social media. He was the only Afghan at the games because the long-standing problems with Afghanistan and the Taliban were at their peak during the Paralympic games. Abbas would have been great at speaking out at this time, but he had to concentrate on swimming. We even advised him to step down from the media so he could focus on his competition.

Right now Abbas is a high profile supporter, and this is a step before becoming a goodwill ambassador. Well-known ambassadors include Cate Blanchett, Stanley Tucci, Kristin Davis, Ben Stiller, Khaled Hosseini, and many others are also part of the UNHCR.

I love how Abbas speaks. His disability is not what shines through but rather his confidence, how he represents people from home, represents refugees, and has a grand sense of responsibility. We are lucky to work with him.

We communicate with him on What's App almost weekly. He sends us pictures, he talks to people in other countries, and we are looking forward to his doing advocacy work with us.

We have helped well over 50 million refugees successfully restart their lives.

Goodwill Ambassadors are some of the most recognizable public faces of UNHCR. They help bring our organization to every corner of the world through their influence and dedication.

ABBAS'S INVOLVEMENT WITH THE UNHCR

We have our meeting on Zoom and we all introduce ourselves. We have an agenda and prepare in advance what we are going to say and what the meeting will be about.

I talk about how sports can affect refugee life. I tell them the story about how sports saved my life. The meetings last for about one hour. I am not a rich celebrity, I am a beginner, but I can be special like they are, and I look forward to being more involved as an ambassador.

Before I left Turkey, I had to take some classes about resettlement and what life was going to be like. Other people in Istanbul were there doing the same thing. I also got health screenings and blood tests to make sure I was healthy. I passed everything and was ready to go.

TEN

COMING TO THE UNITED STATES

> Risk something or forever sit with your dreams.
>
> — Herb Brooks —
>
> U.S.A. ice hockey player and coach who won gold at the 1980 Winter Olympics as the head coach of the famous "Miracle on Ice" team

The Oregon Reign Masters with their 1st place banner.

It was August of 2016 when I found out I was going to the USA. I had only three weeks to prepare. It was one of the happiest days of my life. They sent someone with me on a Turkish Airways flight to Los Angeles. I was so excited I could barely hold a thought in my head. My assistant helped me with my food, with my bags, and with my seatbelt. When the area to sit in is tight, I cannot eat with my feet and I need someone else to feed me. We were the last people to board the plane for this 15-hour flight. My life was about to change.

I remembered when I was a kid wondering how an airplane could fly to the United States…it was so far away. Equally amazing to me was that I was on my way there now. I didn't think much else about the United States. As a kid, it was simply another world with big buildings and pretty girls who showed their faces, legs, feet, and arms. I loved seeing romantic scenes in the movies from there. People talked about September 11th and George Bush, and many times I saw the video from when the World Trade Center was attacked. I didn't understand politics when I was young, but I care about it now and someday I want to be involved in it. People always tell me that I have leadership skills.

In a few hours, the United States would not be a faraway place anymore. When this Turkish Airlines plane landed in Los Angeles, I would be there. I met some Americans at the Turkish camp, and they told me that everyone in America is always busy and people work very long hours.

The first thing I noticed were all of the shiny cars.

When I got to the Los Angeles airport my visa was checked and then I ate my first very salty American chicken and rice dinner.

I slept in a hotel and was wide awake in the middle of the night from jet lag. The next day I flew to Portland, Oregon, and got such a warm welcome. Police were there to greet me, Catholic Charities too; and after all this time, there was Mike. We hugged so hard and for so long. From there I had to sign some official papers. People there tried to look nonchalant as I did the signing with my foot, the pen between my big toe and first toe. This is how I write. Catholic Charities gave me $900 so I had that to add to the money from the UNHCR.

Then we went to Mike's car, and he took me home to his nice house. I felt like my life was going to get really good. Mike seemed as wonderful as I expected. On the ride to Mike's house, I couldn't stop looking at all the new shiny cars. I had never seen most of these cars before.

I was overwhelmed with relief and tiredness and convinced that all the work it took to get here was worth it. I felt as if I would sleep for a week. Mike lived in Gresham, just outside of Portland. It was a big house with three bedrooms, two bathrooms and a big wooden wraparound outdoor deck on a big piece of land just off I-84.

Mike slept in the master bedroom, and the two other bedrooms had bunk beds. For now, I had my own room although four additional people could comfortably live here.

The kitchen was well equipped although Mike was a lousy cook.

The first night I was there he made me a giant sausage to eat that was hard to chew and very salty.

I was ready for things to get easy and fall into place. That did not happen.

Mike was a longtime Portland resident and recently retired as a special education teacher at Centennial High School. He was also a well-respected wrestling coach. First, he watched me swim at a local gym. Through his connections, Mike found a group for me to swim with 20 minutes from his house, the Oregon Reign Masters.

The head coach, Dennis Baker, invited me to join the team. The workouts are posted on a board and the swimmers follow that. Oregon Reign is part of the network of United States Masters swim teams that provide membership benefits to nearly 65,000 masters swimmers in all 50 states. Its 52 Local Masters Swimming Committees (LMSCs) provide direct support to more than 1,500 Masters Swimming clubs and workout groups. Structure and organization of USMS programs vary according to pool availability, instructor or coach availability, community support, and finances. The majority of locations offering Masters Swimming programs have coaches on deck. Coaches write workouts and provide feedback and instruction. Coach Baker put me in my own lane so I was separated from the other swimmers and for a long time I did not meet the other swimmers. He gave me my own workout and I liked it at first. Soon I wanted to race the other swimmers, but that was not easy to orchestrate.

I shaved my head and started running in a nearby park to help my swim times. I also walked to a nearby gym, and I included that in my training. At first I was a little scared to be out in the dark but then I got used to it. It was minor discomfort compared to the much bigger ones I have had.

For a year Mike would drive me to swim practice, often twice a day. After a while he grew tired of doing this and asked me to take the bus, but I insisted that he drive me instead. I had to. I knew that he would never understand why. The bus made me feel as if I were back at the Turkish refugee camp. He got mad at me for asking him to do that but he did it.

Eventually Mike taught me how to drive a car, and I got a permit then a license and started driving myself to practice in his 2003 red Ford Explorer.

One of my Afghan friends in Portland told him that she didn't think it was safe for me to drive, but Mike encouraged me to continue. We made my driving a fun adventure where we would get burgers, Orange Julius, and tuna sandwiches and he would feed me while I was driving.

I suppose driving with my feet looked risky to other people, but what they didn't know is that I have done risky things my entire life. My family was always concerned with my taking risks. Telling me I cannot do something encourages me to do it more. I drive with my left foot on the steering wheel, and the right foot on the floor to control the gas pedal and brakes. It's the position my body has to be in so staying flexible is crucial. It is not comfortable but it is worth it to me to feel independent.

Living with Mike was not an easy living situation, and we argued a lot. I was an angry 19-year-old, and he was advising me on how to do things and I was not listening to him. How could he possibly advise me? No one can know my life, every obstacle I have dealt with, and what I had to break through to open doors for myself. At the same time, I was being judged by other people who always doubted what I could accomplish.

But there were lessons I learned from Mike that I valued. I realized the importance of being nice to other people. I practiced controlling The Beast more because I understood that doing so is better for my future. It also felt good for me to help him. Before he got sick, I would take him to the movies and the eye doctor. His eyesight was failing, and I became his driver in the Ford Explorer.

I cared about Mike and I know that he cared about me. To be honest, I am uncomfortable when people care about me. I don't want advice. Please don't teach me things, I know what I am doing. I have been through so much and have gotten through things. I figured out how to get to Turkey from Kabul. I figured out how to get to the United States. There is something to be said for the way I do things even if your way is better. I want to be respected for my own decisions.

Mike showed me lots of beautiful places in Oregon like the Pacific Ocean and Multnomah Falls. I looked at pictures of this area before I came here, and I already knew that it was green and lush. The downtown looks so manicured and modern. Suburban Gresham felt like a village. I was so happy to be here after all that time in Turkey. I loved Portland, I still love Portland. I will always love Portland.

Mike got on my nerves a lot, and being with him so much was a test of my patience. He would question me about what I was eating when he could see what I was eating. I would get angry, and I found myself frequently apologizing for things I would say to him. He was hard for me to live with and at the same time, I was so deeply grateful for what he had done for me. I lived with Mike for four years and will always consider him my American father. For four years I went to competitions with Mike. He was my caretaker, my assistant, a father figure, and a coach figure. At swim meets, he helped put on my swimsuit and dry off after.

While in Portland, I met three Afghan families who I could speak Dari with, a comforting little piece of home for me. Sometimes I slept over at their houses, and we would eat traditional Afghan foods together. Mike welcomed the Afghan community into his home.

As much as people tried to help me, I was still full of anger. I needed someone to rely on, and I always felt like no one deeply cared about me. How could they? These are new people in my life, we are just getting to know each other. Yes, I have my family on the other side of the world and I know that they care about me, but here, alone with strangers, I realize that as strong as I am I still need help with my life. I called my parents and my four brothers almost every day to check on them.

Connecting with the Afghan community helped me adjust to life here but the only thing that really kept me centered in my new life was swimming. Swimming was really the only consistency in my life. Well, swimming and God. I am guided by God and talk to him often during prayer three times a day, in the morning, afternoon, and before bed. I use the prayer rug that I carried with me from Kabul. Someday I will get a new rug and hang the rug that I have carried all this time on the wall to remind me of my journey.

When I swim, I think about what is good for me. I realize from getting older, that fighting is not good for me. In the midst of my bravado and boldness, I am lonely. I think about my next five years and I listen to music to put my brain in a positive place. I must do these things or I will be mad and angry all the time, and The Beast will take over. The focus helps me use my anger as motivation and channel it into swimming.

I think about my life all the time. If I were rich I would go back home, have sheep, cows, and goats, and live a simple life with no internet. I would have a donkey and ride horses in the mountains. I want to eventually get off social media and stop being famous and let go of the pressure and responsibility that comes with that. Karizak is the small village where my father is from. My family would go there to relax and enjoy the total quietness. The only thing you hear is the river next to where he lived. I would be happy there. When women and men and disabled people are equal I can go back to Afghanistan but that will be later.

For now, I must swim faster and be number one. That goal puts a lot of pressure on me but I see using my ability as a gift from God.

During the time I lived in Portland I got more involved with the UNHCR. I have made public service videos about my story for them and I speak to refugees about the importance of sport.

I want to give back to others for how they helped me. I do whatever they want me to do. It is a lofty and important job and I am proud to be a part of it. Usually around 20 people are at our Zoom meetings. We follow an agenda after introducing ourselves.

I was invited twice to Geneva, Switzerland, as part of the Global Youth Advisory Council to speak at the High Commissioner's

Dialogue on Protection Challenges. I used my passion for swimming as a way to advocate for the positive impact swimming has had on my life as a displaced person with a disability. I talked about how sports affects the lives of refugees.

> *Sport keeps you emotionally and mentally strong.*
> *Sport keeps your body in good physical condition.*
> *Sport keeps you away from weed, tobacco, and alcohol.*
> *Once you become proficient at a sport, you become an example for others. By being that example, you can bring necessary changes.*

Mike went to Geneva with me both times, and we stayed for a week in a nice hotel. He fed me on the airplane. I had to be prepared with my ideas and my talk and memorize things. Right now, I am so proud to be a youth advisor.

Although I need money and this is not a paid position, I knew that I had a lot to offer the UNHCR and that this connection would somehow benefit me. They are the reason I am here now. Many times my life was just too hard and I wanted to return to Kabul, give up swimming and just go home.

Soon I hope to be a US citizen, and then I can be something bigger than I am now, a role model for other refugees with the power to help Afghanistan in some way.

Now that I was a regular swimmer with Oregon Reign, I started competing again and winning in swim meets. I saw myself as a champion. This is Coach Dennis Baker's perspective:

DENNIS BAKER
Head Coach, Oregon Reign Masters

I knew about Mike Ives before I met him. He had a good reputation as coach and teacher. He sought me out and thought that our masters swim team was the right place for Abbas. The monthly fee is $62, but I gave Abbas a full scholarship. I mean, how do you charge a guy with a story like his? I didn't have expectations of Abbas when I met him. I have worked with disabled people my whole life and know that they never wanted to be treated differently from the other swimmers. I never saw Abbas as disabled. Had there been no pandemic, Abbas would have stayed in Portland. I met some of his Afghan friends and I could see how he excelled at being a voice for refugees.

Abbas quickly bonded with the other swimmers; they loved him. At the end-of-the-year banquet, he got multiple awards and was a team high point scorer. In 2017 Abbas went to the Mexico World Para Swimming Championships and saw his swimming career take off with a silver medal for the 50-meter butterfly. At his second World Championship in London in 2019, he finished sixth in the 50m butterfly.

I had Abbas with our team for three years when the pandemic came and shut everything down, which meant I had no pool to give him. I am the executive director of three pools, but my swimmers had to travel to swim and availability was erratic. I didn't want Abbas to be a pool refugee.

It broke my heart when Abbas's father died that year and he went back to Kabul. I stayed awake all night worrying about him. I was afraid we would never see Abbas again. He could have been sent to prison or worse, but he was so confident that nothing would happen to him and he was right.

Two of my coaches, brother and sister Allen and Linda Larson knew Coach Marty Hendrick in Fort Lauderdale. The pools there remained open, and Abbas was invited to come train there. This was the best situation for Abbas. He understood what he needed to do.

My love and admiration for Abbas is big, and when you feel this way about someone it is not hard to let them go.

Mike's Deteriorating Health

A year after Mike got sick I knew that he was going to die. He had heart problems, eye problems, and kidney problems. He was overweight and could not stop eating. I tried to help him with overeating but I could not. I came back to Portland from Fort Lauderdale to take care of him. By then, Mike had kidney failure and was not doing well. He was ready to die, but he brightened up when I arrived to help him.

Mike Ives died in February of 2022.

Mike's lifelong friend, Steve Heintz tells his story

> ABBAS IS SO CHARISMATIC...HE THINKS HE CAN DO EVERYTHING...
> AND FOR THE MOST PART, HE IS RIGHT.
> I WAS THERE FROM THE TIME MIKE FIRST SAW ABBAS ON FACEBOOK.

I met Abbas when he first arrived from Turkey. At first he was quiet and shy but made friends easily and people liked him right away so he adjusted quickly. He was constantly dazzled at the variety of restaurants and all the different kinds of food available in Portland. His life here must have seemed like a kingdom to him compared to the refugee camps. Mike spent a lot of time and money getting Abbas here, and the members of the Rockwood Seventh-Day Adventist Church were a good support team.

I could see right away that Abbas was a strong-willed person. Mike and Abbas were both religious, Abbas is a Shiite Muslim and Mike was a Seventh-Day Adventist. Each of them would stick up for what they believed, but Mike took the role of the Dad and often they butted heads. Although Mike had sponsored other refugees, this was the first time he dealt with the United Nations. When he had sponsored other promising young disabled people, he dealt with Catholic Charities. Mike's church helped him with all the necessary legal documents. He learned how to work with the UNHCR and how to navigate through the complicated and often frustrating procedures. He was often told NO, but he never gave up. He kept in contact every night with Abbas, and he was encouraged that this was going to happen. Through his confidence Abbas became encouraged too.

I met Mike Ives 40 years ago when I was 16 and Mike was coaching wrestling. He paired up the wrestling bracket and studied who was the best combination to wrestle. Mike had a sixth sense about how to do this and was usually right.

Mike was my coach and had been a coach for his entire adult life. At 74, he was meticulously organized and great with technical things and computers.

I was born in 1964, and our friendship blossomed through our mutual interest in wrestling. He wrestled while growing up in Bismarck, North Dakota. He used to talk about being raised on a chicken farm and how he hated it and how he was glad to be moving to Portland after graduating college in 1969. Mike got a job as a special education teacher and worked with hearing impaired students in the Portland Public School District. He would travel from school to school to wherever the impaired students needed him.

Although Mike had two sisters and a brother in Washington, they were not close to him, but they were close to each other. Mike was an outcast and did not include them in his will. When he died, whatever he had, he left to the kids he helped.

Everyone knew Mike. He published the *Oregon Wrestling Record* with all the statistics from every high school and every tournament. He spent a lot of time on this and had a lot of time because he never had a wife or kids of his own.

Mike was also a Boy Scout troop leader and loved going on camping trips with the kids. He did this for more than 30 years, and he impacted the lives of so many people. Mike treated all the kids he dealt with like they were his own. Yes, he was a terrible cook, but the kids did the cooking and Mike would cut up the food for the kids who could not cut their own.

Mike handled everything in a meticulous systematic way. In 2017 when Abbas left the country to compete in Mexico City, and again in London in 2019, we were afraid that he would not be able to come back in because of his refugee status. Mike Ives worked out the details beforehand and there never was a problem. When Abbas returned to Kabul after his father died, again we were concerned that he would not come back. Mike made sure it went smoothly.

He had a keen sense of who he could help and who he could bring to his home. Mike communicated with each person intensely on the computer to size up their situation. Although it was always a risk, he was never disappointed.

Abbas was not his first disabled kid, there were many. Mike also found Julian Molina on the computer. Julian is a one-legged BMX rider from Andes, Colombia, who lived there for a while. Molina lost his leg in a car accident, and Mike helped him get a prosthetic leg from Shriners. Mike took a special interest in people from other countries and looked for people to help. He would see videos of different young people and made contact with them.

Mike also helped Michael Trimble, a one-time candidate for governor of Oregon. He has no arms, and lived with Mike for two years. They butted heads on politics and saw the world differently. Trimble was able to eventually go out on his own with help from Catholic Charities.

Mike also took in a set of twins who were wrestlers that he let live in his house, Roy and Lupi Sanchez. They needed financial help and were from 50 miles away at Glendale High School. Now, one is a chiropractor and one is a teacher.

Mike never wanted recognition for what he did. He had the skills to help and he did it because it was the right thing to do.

Mike was overweight, a diabetic, and his heart was failing. He also had kidney failure. He was not going to do dialysis, but the kids talked him into it. Mike's goal was to see Abbas become an American citizen, but he died before that happened. He did know that Abbas made the Paralympic team and was going to compete in Tokyo. He was afraid that Abbas would be sent back to Turkey because his visa was running out and he called every politician he knew to help him.

Mike felt sad when Abbas moved to Florida but he knew it was the best decision for him. He could only go so far with his training here since there were no swimming pools open. Florida had what he needed.

I was like family to Mike, and I am the executor of Mike's will. His house is for sale now with an asking price of $574,586. When it sells, the money will go to the kids he helped, including Abbas.

Mike kept a diary about our experiences, here is part of what he said:

THIS IS PART OF A DIARY MIKE IVES KEPT ABOUT ABBAS:

I always wanted to be a national coach but never dreamed it would be as a swim coach for an armless swimmer. I don't know much about swimming and I can barely swim but helping Abbas gave me an appreciation for the sport. I read things online on how to coach swimming but I am a wrestling coach so I could only do so much. I have been watching Dennis Baker at work coaching the Oregon Reign Masters so I picked up a few tips there.

His advice to me as the novice coach? Tell him not to go out too hard at the start. With that advice, how can Abbas Karimi possibly lose? Ha!

Our first competition in 2016 was a local meet in Augusta GA where Abbas won the 50-meter butterfly, the 50-meter freestyle and the 50-meter backstroke.

MEXICO CITY

"I was trying to smile but my lips were shaking, my body was shaking. I'm standing there thinking about how I'm representing 80 million displaced people from around the world. I'm the only refugee to ever win an international title like this. I made history. But I'm also thinking, I'm not done"

- Abbas Karimi on winning the silver medal

Next was Mexico City to the 2017 World Paralympic Championships which Abbas had qualified for in Indianapolis last June. Most of the expenses were picked up by International Paralympic Association IPA Swimming which was great, but they gave us essentially no rest or acclimation time before the swimming began. I am sure this must have been because there had been a lot of non-recoverable expenses from the postponement and then later rescheduling the meet after the terrible earthquake that shook this city just before the originally scheduled meet in September. No one mentioned this, but it seems logical. I served as a co-team leader for the independent para team, while a very knowledgeable Greek 2004 Olympian Alex Tsoltos served as my counterpart.

Anyway, the elevation took its toll on Abbas, but he handled it well. Early in the meet, he got the silver medal in the S5 50m butterfly. First place went to a fine young man from Turkey who had previously been Abbas's teammate while Abbas was in Turkey. He not only won the S5 50-meter butterfly event, but also the 50-meter freestyle overall title.

ABBAS IS CLASSIFIED AS AN S5 SWIMMER. HERE IS WHAT THAT MEANS:

When Abbas and I went to Indianapolis in 2017 he was assigned an S5 classification in all of his strokes and remains an S5 swimmer.

This is how he got that classification: The International Paralympic Committee (IPC) made Abbas swim all four strokes. They timed him, watched his flip turn and measured him. One person on the committee must have a medical background. Abbas must be assigned this classification to compete internationally and I think that the system is fair. Abbas does his part by staying in the best shape that he can. He knows most of the other S5 swimmers, there are about 15-20 of them, and they are friends. Now there are new younger ones coming up.

Basically, para-swimming classification is designed so that disabled swimmers can have fair competition.

Some swimmers compete in one class for one stroke and a different class for another stroke because different strokes require the use of different muscle groups. In the breaststroke hands and hips play a crucial role. It also means that swimmers with cerebral palsy, spinal cord injuries and limb deficiencies can compete against each other.

The classification system was originally based on medical criteria, but is now largely based on functional disability to make para-swimming more competitive. The classes are prefixed with "S" for freestyle, butterfly and backstroke events, "SB" for breaststroke and "SM" for individual medley events. Swimmers with physical disabilities are divided into ten classes based on their degree of functional disability: S1, S2, S3, S4, S5, S6, S7, S8, S9 and S10. The lower number indicates a greater degree of impairment. Those with visual impairments are placed in three additional classes: S11, S12 and S13. One more class, S14, is reserved for swimmers with intellectual impairment. A final class, S15, is for athletes with hearing loss.

The general rules for Paralympic swimming are based on rules for able-bodied competitors. The rules regarding strokes, turns and the length of time that swimmers may remain under water are similar to those for the Olympic Games.

The first classification system for para-swimming was created during the 1940s when swimmers were classified based on their medical conditions. In an effort to clearly describe disabilities and promote fairness, the number of classifications ballooned and that made organizing competitive events difficult because there were too few people in each classification and as many winners as competitors. At the 1988 Summer Paralympics in Seoul, the number of eligible classes was so great that 60 gold medals were awarded in one swimming event.

The reality is that able bodied athletes get more attention and more sponsorships because more people watch them. The world is starting to pay more attention to para-athletes but it has a ways to go.

Abbas came away with one of the 30 gold medals (15 men, 15 women) that were awarded. He had an outstanding performance. Norman Santos came with us on the trips to help out. He lives at my home too, he was from the Phillipines and he did not have arms. He likes to cook and mostly makes the food that he grew up with: Spanish Asian American influenced food. I also met him on the internet through a friend in Texas who is Filipino and brought Norman here and I took him to live with me. Norman speaks broken English and is not an American citizen. He was also getting help from the UNHCR but they dropped him because he did not show up for appointments. We tried to get them to give him another chance but they had to move on to help someone else. Norman tried to take the driver's test and he can drive a little bit but he cannot pass the written test. Norman does not have Abbas's precision and drive.

I gave Norman money too, and although I was never very cautious about any of these people who I opened my home to, it has always worked out.

I am proud to know Abbas and if I had a son of my own I would be happy if it were him.

Abbas wants to be an American citizen and a Paralympic champion. I am certain that he can do both.

Tonight, Abbas came to a high school wrestling meet at David Douglas High School with me and a few of my friends. Some young Turkish men sat down in front of us. When Abbas heard them speaking Turkish, he told them he lived in Turkey for four years. They made it clear they did not want to talk to Abbas and I assumed it was because of old negative feelings between Turks and Afghans.

Abbas said no. They said they did not want to talk to any armless boy. I wish I had learned this before leaving the gym. These two boys had obviously not accepted the principles by which we now live in the USA. Just because they have arms and Abbas has none does not make them better than him. Their attitude makes them much worse.

The way I see it, Abbas, you lost a chance to practice your Turkish, but they lost the opportunity to meet you and learn some of the things you could teach them. My thoughts are that God loves them a little less for their thoughtlessness and loves you a little more for forgiving and loving them.

Abbas, don't let jerks like those two ever slow you down. You are much better than they can ever hope to be. Everyone who knows you is proud to be part of your life.

LONDON

It is time I quit putting off writing about my trip to London with Abbas for the World Paralympic meet. I was again the refugee team coach. When we landed at Heathrow we were met by Sangwoo, a representative of the International Paralympic Committee. We boarded a bus to Mama Shelter, a brand new hotel that was nice in a spartan kind of way.

The 2019 competition was held at the site of the 2012 Olympics.

Abbas had solid times in freestyle, butterfly and backstroke and qualified for Tokyo.

He beat his old teammate, Beytullah of Turkey who edged him out for the world title in Mexico City, 2017. That renewed his strong desire to win gold in Tokyo.

We never did see any of the sites in London, I was too tired from all the walking and Abbas was too tired from swimming. Still, Abbas toured the sites in London with a childhood friend who lived there.

It felt good to be coaching again, even in a sport I know so little about. I never had world placers in wrestling so this was an ego boost for me even if the credit really belongs with Dennis Baker.

The last meet for Abbas while he was in Portland was in Indianapolis and Abbas placed in the 100m freestyle, the first time he has participated in that event for a couple years.

Finding a place for Abbas to change into and out of a swimsuit was a challenge. With Larry Nassar, the rogue doctor molesting young girls in gymnastics, swimming implemented new changes about the supervision of adults working with not only the youth but adult athletes.

A PERSONAL LOSS FOR ABBAS

Several days after the 2019 World Championships in London, England, my father died. I went back to Afghanistan for 11 days to be with my mother. I cried so much during this time. It cost me so much to try to become a Paralympic champion. So many times I wanted to quit after I put myself on this path, I gave up everything. My father said, "I knew when you were born that you were going to be something special. Among all my kids, all my sons and daughters, you're the only one who put my name on top of the world."

I always wanted to make my father proud of me. I came into Mike's room at 3 a.m. to tell him, and I was just devastated. My close Afghan friend, Saifullah, was sleeping on the couch that night and was able to give me comfort in my own language. I arrived in Portland on Monday, and was on a flight home on Friday."

When I think about my father I see this: He is sitting next to me cutting apples and giving me some of the pieces and eating some himself too. He was going to be getting surgery and people had come to see him and brought him fruit and juice. I wish he would have lived to see me go to the Paralympics in Tokyo.
My father was emotional. He had high expectations of me, and he knew that I would be something. My father was stubborn. He ate what he wanted to eat, not what he should have eaten, and he was like me, the king of his life. Maybe I will be different and do things the American way.

He didn't live long enough but he lived to know that I was going to be a champion. Somewhere, he is proud of me.

I have to have a better life, and I am representing all the other refugees who want the same thing.

I know that my mother is proud of me. I do a lot of things my way, but I am still her Afghan boy. I am both.

I will never quit on my dreams. The Beast would never allow that.

MARK PINGER
MARKETING REPRESENTATIVE, ARENA SWIMWEAR

Arena Swimwear is one of Abbas's sponsors.
Mark Pinger explains how that happened:

I am a refugee too, from Germany, and working on becoming a US citizen. I met Abbas at a swim meet at Mt. Hood Community College Aquatic Center in early 2019 before the pandemic.

I am a masters swimmer too, and I am also the marketing representative for Arena swimwear. I saw that Abbas was wearing Arena goggles, the expensive $70 ones, so I already knew that he liked the brand.

I introduced myself and told him that I was inspired by his swimming and that he inspires a lot of other people too.

We had never met before. The meeting was not more than that, and then we started texting. Abbas posts a lot on his social media and has lots of followers. I also noticed that in his pictures he is usually wearing Arena suits and apparel.

I told him I would provide him with anything he wants to try or needs. At Arena, we put a lot into our athletes and give them things to try. We gave him a suit with a USA flag on it but it was not until he became a citizen that he wore it.

Arena used to be part of Adidas until the mid-1990s when we became a separate company. We are smaller in the United States than we are in Europe. Many of the Olympians and Paralympians who wear our brand are from Europe, and we are based in Tolentino, Italy.

Jessica Long was the first Paralympic athlete we sponsored and we still have a relationship with her.

Another former Olympian we signed is Mark Spitz.

We also decided to make Abbas a representative. There is no formal contract, he is just a great ambassador for our brand. When Abbas does good for himself, it is also good for Arena.

To me, Abbas's disability is hard to relate to, but having a tough day is very relatable, he just has had a lot more of them.

I saw Abbas again at the Golden Goggle awards in Miami, and I got to meet his coach, Marty Hendrick. It makes me happy that The Golden Goggles Awards exposes Paralympic athletes too.

The Golden Goggles recognizes and honors accomplishments of swimmers who represent the United States, an honor that started in 2004 by USA Swimming Foundation.

There are eight main categories: Breakout Performer of the Year, Coach of the Year, Perseverance Award, Relay Performance of the Year, Male Race of the Year, Female Race of the Year, Male Athlete of the Year, and Female Athlete of the Year. Nominees in each category are announced in advance of the awards ceremony and recipients of each award are revealed at the formal black tie ceremony itself. Winners for each award are determined by a selection panel and fan votes. The awards ceremony is also a fundraiser for the foundation, with seats and tables available for purchase and proceeds going to the foundation and other humanitarian efforts such as aid relief for those affected by Hurricane Katrina.

I got to be part of the ceremony. The event was held in Miami Beach at the Faena Hotel. I loved getting all dressed up to introduce Breastsroker/IM Lilly King

ALLEN LARSON

I was Abbas's coach, fellow swimmer, and friend. I am a USMS Level 3 coach and an assistant coach to Dennis Baker. I met Mike Ives during the time he was driving Abbas to swim practice. He was hoping I would eventually take Abbas on the swim trips, and I was excited to do that but COVID-19 stopped it all. Mike was struggling with his health and Abbas needed more of a coach than he was. Getting Abbas to train is not a problem. Getting him to back off of training is. He is razor focused.

When the pandemic closed the pools, Dennis and I rattled our connections to find places to swim. Some of them were an hour's travel time away so that Abbas could swim for just 45 minutes. We did that three days a week. I would drive to the Chehalem Aquatic Center in Newberg to use a 25-yard 8-lane pool during the height of COVID-19. I would take Abbas and create workouts for him. Dennis wanted me to do this, and I wanted to do it too.

I had a friend a 10-hour drive away in southern Oregon. Since we got pool time every day, we stayed there for a while and I coached him.

Me, Abbas, and my sister, Linda, went to Folsom, California, to swim. He loved when Linda coached him. She orchestrated her practices like Coach Marty Hendrick's practices. That is when she came up with the idea of Abbas staying at her place in Fort Lauderdale for a couple of weeks and swimming with Marty's team, Swim Fort Lauderdale Masters.

My sister Linda is a world class, All-American, national record holder swimmer and a Level 3 certified masters swim coach.

Although she and I grew up in Portland, she is a flight attendant with American Airlines and is in Fort Lauderdale often enough to have a home there, very close to the Fort Lauderdale Aquatic Complex. She swims in Portland and in Fort Lauderdale and has competed for Swim Fort Lauderdale since 2007

LINDA LARSON

I am a backup coach and offer to coach when I am needed. I follow Marty's workouts and I also use much of his style when I coach. I talk to the swimmers during the practice. I help them with sendoffs, because sometimes watching the clock gets confusing. I compliment the swimmers if it is appropriate. I stay engaged for the entire practice like Marty does. When I compete, I swim for Swim Fort Lauderdale.

I grew up in Portland and have known Dennis Baker since we were six years old.

While training with Oregon Reign Masters in 2016, I met Abbas. Dennis gave him his own lane, and Abbas would train on his own.

Dennis has a totally different coaching style from Marty. Dennis gives the lanes their workouts and their intervals but does not interact with the swimmers while they are swimming. The lanes are organized according to speed level.

Abbas does not read the clock and sometimes is not sure when to go. Dennis does not correct strokes during practice and has his own side hustle teaching stroke. He calls the workout and that is it. One thing that is really cool about swimming outside in Portland, during the winter there is snow on the ground and the pool water is warm. It is surreal to see the steam rising from the pool.

When Abbas just arrived here from Turkey, this was all new for him. He blended in socially with the team but swam alone and did his own thing. I used to see Mike Ives when he brought Abbas to practice; he was there all the time.

But Coach Baker did not have the time to work individually with Abbas, so my brother, Allen Larson, became his trainer.

Allen was offered the trip to Tokyo with Abbas and time to get him ready for the Paralympics. Allen had to get aggressive to find pool time since, by March 2020, the pools had closed down.

Had there been no pandemic, I assessed the situation and this was my concern: Allen was dedicated but he did not have the patience or the knowledge or the experience to get Abbas to the Paralympics.

The three of us were in the car driving to the Chehalem pool in Newberg, and Abbas asked if I would do the workout for him on that day. I told him that I would just give him Marty's workout. Then I suggested he go to Fort Lauderdale, stay in my condo, and swim with Marty. The pools stayed open in Fort Lauderdale during COVID-19. I reminded him that all the time that I coached him I did so using Marty's workouts. I reminded Allen that when he came to train with Marty before a meet in Puerto Rico, he had his best times ever.

I know Marty well and I was certain that having Abbas as a project would also be good for Marty. The pandemic left Marty isolated, and he needed a challenge.

It was a huge undertaking for Marty and he certainly did not need to take this on for more accolades or additions to his resume. Abbas would get the training he needed with Marty. Marty had coached Justin Zook, a Paralympic athlete in 2011 and had a wide range of swimming connections.

Marty was a master at human relations, and he would get Abbas to the Paralympics, he would get Abbas his US citizenship, and he would get Abbas his world record. And he did.

The timing was right.

Abbas had to move on, and I felt secure in this plan.

I also knew that the SFTL team would embrace Abbas and Abbas said early on that he felt like he was on a team.

Marty engages. He knows everyone's names and something about them. He has a way of making you feel that you are the only person there. Swimmers love that. Actually, who doesn't love that?

It was this sentence, "Why don't you train with Marty for a couple of weeks?" that changed the trajectory of Abbas's life.

The atmosphere of the SFTL team is different too. We communicate with each other. We are social. This all comes from Marty. For example, Abbas did not just show up one day and start swimming with the team. An introductory email was sent out, and swimmers were waiting for him:

> *I am very excited to introduce a new member to Swim Fort Lauderdale, Abbas Karimi. Abbas is coming to Fort Lauderdale to continue his preparation for the 2021 Paralympic Games in Tokyo, which starts in one year, August 24, 2021.*
>
> *Abbas is an amazing young man and a true example of overcoming life's many obstacles and working towards higher goals. I guess he is the definition of a true champion. He will be spending a lot of time around the Carter Aquatic Complex, so I thought each of you might benefit from knowing*

a little bit about him. His first day of workouts with SFTL Masters will be this Thursday,

Please welcome him (at a minimum of 6 feet and with your mask on) when you see him at the pool.

Now Abbas would be sharing lanes with other swimmers, something he did not do in Portland

All I can say is that you hear all these American Dream stories and they are pretty farfetched. Except for Abbas; his American dream came true.

MIKE IVES' LAST DIARY ENTRY:

ABBAS IS MOVING ON

It is a sad day today. Abbas is moving to Florida in a few hours.

It will be a happy day when Abbas moves back to Portland after the Olympics with his gold medal in hand. Florida is a good move for him. He can get in as many as three practices a day there with top-notch coaching. The pools are all outside so it will be easier to battle COVID-19. We will both stay strong with our Gods and our faith.

Wish you the best of futures, my brother and son. Stay strong in your faith in our mutual God.

Mike.

ELEVEN

A MOVE TO FORT LAUDERDALE

SWIMMING IS THE ANSWER.
THE QUESTION IS PRETTY MUCH IRRELEVANT.

Marty and Abbas share a laugh.

When I first got here on August 26th, 2020, it was strange how the land was so flat and everything on it was so hot. We swim here in competition pools that have to be chilled to around 77-82 degrees. Without chillers, swimmers here would tire very quickly in warm water. Water that is too warm can cause a rapid decrease in blood pressure and that can lead to dizziness or loss of consciousness.

I already knew that Fort Lauderdale had nice beaches and basically two seasons, hot and warm. It was prettier than I thought it would be although I know I am living in the prettiest part of this area. I see the ocean, the inland waterways, boats, and swimming pools everywhere. Everything around where my coach lives is so nice.

The swimmers welcomed me. They all knew about me before and introduced themselves to me at my first practice. I had something to offer them too:

I know that I influence the other swimmers, they look up to me. I give them an extra push just by being who I am.

I don't try to influence, I just keep working on myself and that becomes the influence. They reconsider some of their excuses and put more effort into their swimming when they see me do it.

Since the aquatic complex is still under construction, we have to use smaller city pools for practice. Seeing all of these nice cars, big houses, and things to buy keeps me motivated to win the gold medal because one day I will have those things too.

All of this luxury taps into the part of me that likes to dress up and show off. This shot of confidence is new for me. I have spent most of my life plenty humble before I became an American. One thing I learned from coming here is that there are lots of opportunities for me. I can do anything. All that I have gone through has prepared me, and my experience has made me unique and more confident.

I remember when I met the Americans while I was still in Turkey, and they told me that everyone in America works very hard. Maybe it is just because I live in Fort Lauderdale but people here have money for cocktails at bars and a lot of free time to drink there and have fun. Fun is a high priority, and swimmers are always getting together and going out to restaurants, bars, shopping, beaches. I have a lot of fun here, and people I meet don't seem to have any shortage of money. Although I have always loved the mountains, this flat hot place is really fabulous.

I go out in groups a lot instead of one-on-one dates. The women who I am exposed to seem so aggressive. Maybe I am not meant for them...our cultures are so different.

I fell into a routine. I was not surprised that I made the refugee Paralympic team, I was the only one with the .38-second butterfly qualifying time, but when it was official I was so excited that I did not sleep for three nights. All I could think about was what I needed to do to win.

The purpose of having a refugee team is to get recognition for refugees and our team had six of them and 26 Olympians. I had the opportunity to win the medal for myself but also for the 82 million refugees. There were six of us on the team, one woman and five men, Ibrahim Al Hussein, Alia Issa, Parfait Hakizimana, Sharhrad Nasajpour, Anas Al Khalifa and me. I was the only swimmer.

Everything was on me and I felt a lot of pressure. I was really comfortable living with Marty. Since Marty is both a swimmer and a coach, he understands me as a swimmer. He is really both a friend and a father figure to me. I loved Mike Ives, but living with him was so much more difficult.

I decided to stay and train in Fort Lauderdale because of Marty. Besides, the pandemic prevented pools from being open anywhere else. He and I made a year's agreement for me to stay here, and we got used to each other. Marty likes having company, and we have created a bond, actually, it's more than a bond—it's a little family. I need his support even though sometimes he doesn't understand the extent I must go to take care of my family. We don't argue, there is no struggle. We respect each other. I will always love him; he has done so much for me. He is so kind and nice to other people and does his best all the time to help. He has a big heart and is a good person, he doesn't try to be that way, he just is that way.

I am not as good of a person as Marty is. I am not as nice. That is not who I am.

What I like about being on SFTL is that I am not seen as a person who cannot do things. I feel equal and that is what I was looking for when I left Kabul: to be an equal.

I am also glad to help SFTL be in the spotlight. I can always say that I got famous here on that team. A lot of my future plans are created here, and my teammates have helped me with that.

By July 20, 2021, I was invited to a Fort Lauderdale city council meeting, and they announced that July 20 will be Abbas Karimi day in recognition and appreciation for my role in the Paralympic games. What an honor to be recognized by city officials.

I was also recognized during the International Day for Persons with Disabilities in 2021 and was featured on UNHCR global social media channels. I spoke about the power of sport and how much it has impacted my life.

I call my family almost every day around 4 a.m. There is a 10-hour time difference. I call one family member per day. They were in Attock, Pakistan, a place where many Afghans resettled when the Taliban took over. This historical town is 70 kilometers west of Islamabad. Many Afghans brought their rug weaving skills and created new lives there. My family stayed about a year, then returned to Kabul. It was too hard for them to make a living there.

LOSING MIKE

Just a few months after I got to Fort Lauderdale Mike Ives's health declined with complications, and I returned to Portland to take care of him. With Norman, we cleaned his house, made food for him, helped him walk and took him outside. We made sure he was clean and had his medicine. We changed his diaper. Then I had to return to Fort Lauderdale. I am glad I was able to repay a tiny bit of what he did for me. I know how much it mattered to him that I was there. Eventually we had hospice people take over.

Norman remained in Portland and lived with people from Mike's Seventh-Day Adventist Church of Portland.

Mike died a few weeks later. I am glad he got to know before he died that I had made the Paralympic team. I will always remember what Mike said about me in his diary: "If I had a son like Abbas, I would be so proud."

This is his obituary:

Michael R. Ives

June 7, 1947 - Jan. 15, 2022

Michael Randolph "Mike" Ives died Jan. 15, 2022 after complications from diabetes. Mike was born in Bismarck, N.D.

He generously supported athletes, the disabled, refugees, and those in need. Mike was a father figure to many and taught in special education in Portland for decades. Many met Mike through wrestling. After being an All-American for Minot State College, Mike coached for Lincoln High School for many years and archived results, ratings, and articles for his Oregon Wrestling Record publication.

Mike is survived by his sisters, Diane Kauk, Marilyn Erickson; and brother, Doug Ives. His parents, Frank and Shirley (Peggy) preceded his death.

MARTY, MOVIES, AND ME

Marty and I watch a lot of movies, at least one per day. We go to sleep very early and we are up before 4 a.m. Swim practices start at 5:30 a.m. That new aquatic center is very close by but it won't be open for a while so we drive to other city pools.

Movies are really my language and culture classes. I have learned so much from movies about style, values, morals, and history. Some of my favorite movies are the James Bond movies. I was introduced to the superhero for the first time in 2016, during the time I was in the fourth refugee camp in Turkey. I saw a James Bond movie in a theater and for me, it went beyond just liking James Bond, I wanted to be James Bond. Once I came to the US I saw all of the James Bond movies.

Maybe I am already a little like James Bond. He and I are focused on our goals. He can also easily eliminate bad people and of course we are both very handsome. Bond is a true gentleman with nice suits. I like the way he drives nice cars and can have any woman he wants. I didn't know about James Bond in Afghanistan but I have learned these things from his movies about being a gentleman. For example, this is what I have to do to be like James Bond. I want to make these things part of me.

- You don't talk about conquests
- You don't clash in public
- You open the door
- You pay the bill
- Be humble. Remember where you come from
- Deliver compliments
- Take responsibility

- Respect other people
- You don't respond to rudeness.
- You bring out the best in everyone.
- You bring out the interesting parts in others.
- Rocky, Bruce Lee, Jason Statham, Rambo, Jackie Chan, Jet Li, Wesley Snipes, Vin Diesel, Arnold Schwarzenegger—I love them all.

TWELVE
MARTY (PART II)

My immediate answer was NO!!! Absolutely not! God no. Hell no. Please no. No way. Nada. No chance. Not in a million years. Never.

He never graduated high school, his English is limited, I am terrible with accents, and my hearing is not that great so I have to read lips a lot, and now it's the pandemic and everyone wears masks and it is even harder for me. I have had enough recognition. I don't need this. Can I just be left off the radar?

My video chat with Abbas changed that. He was articulate, confident, engaging, and we connected immediately. Then I saw the video of him swimming, and I was hooked. Ultimately, his dreams of becoming a Paralympian also became my dreams.

— Marty Hendrick —

It all started when Allen Larson sent me a random email that said, "How would you like a feather in your coaching cap and a free trip to Tokyo? He told me about Abbas and sent a bio video.

I read this email at 5 a.m. before 5:30 a.m. swim practice, then I read it aloud to the other people there and I watched the video of him swimming. Allen's sister Linda is one of my swimmers and volunteer coaches. I also knew Allen through swim meets and his visits here.

My curiosity about the video of Abbas swimming got the best of me and I wanted to know what kind of life Abbas had led so I called Linda Larson. Linda is an American Airlines flight attendant and goes back and forth from Portland to Fort Lauderdale and swims with both Oregon Reign and Swim Fort Lauderdale. She told me how her brother Allen and Abbas were traveling around desperately looking for pool time because the pandemic was shutting everything down. Sometimes they drove eight hours to get in an hour swim. Linda wasn't sure why they didn't just come to Fort Lauderdale and stay in her condo here and use her car. Unlike the rest of the country, the pools here stayed open.

I thought maybe I would organize a two-week training camp for Abbas.

The first thing I did was comb my swimming contacts for some direction, and wrote this email:

Hey Jeanine,

I am getting a new swimmer who is training for the Tokyo Paralympics in 2021.

He will be swimming under the International Refugee flag. He is an S5 swimmer originally from Afghanistan. He fled there at the age of 16 and is currently in Portland OR. Linda Larson, one of my swimmers and volunteer coaches, is in Portland a lot with her mother and has swam with Abbas at Oregon Reign. She says I can help him achieve his goals.

I know my limits on the understanding of the "politics & requirements" for the games and can use your help.

Can I count on you?

Marty Hendrick

Head Masters Coach
Swim Fort Lauderdale "SFTL"
2014, 2015, 2016 & 2017 U.S. Masters Swimming Club National Champions
2015 U.S Masters Swimming Club of the Year

Abbas and I started texting. For him to stay at Linda Larson's condo added another complication so I invited him to stay with me.

Soon after he arrived I was captivated, just like everyone else when they meet him. What an honor and blessing to have met him. Abbas carries an aura like some kind of prophet for the disabled and refugees and it makes me think that he has been placed here to speak about a lot of things. He already has people look at him as their representative. I forget that he is handicapped. It is like race, sometimes you see beyond skin color, and it is like that with Abbas.

You have good athletes and elite athletes. His focus, his interest, was to get faster. He was a champion already in so many ways, and he had unfinished business to complete.

I looked at working with Abbas simply this way: he is another swimmer and I am a coach. My job is to prepare him to swim faster than he did before, and I had a whole group of coaches and swimmers working with me.

This method has always worked for me. I was naïve.

This was the Tokyo Paralympics.

I looked at Olympian Caleb Dressel and what he said about the magnanimity of what he was doing, "It's just another swim meet." And that put it all in a manageable perspective for me.

I had space in my home for him, an extra bedroom, and an extra bathroom. I come from a large family and was raised to always have a place for houseguests.

I was both excited and apprehensive about this new journey. When I started SFTL masters in 2005 that was a new journey. Back then we started with nine swimmers at the iconic but very worn out Fort Lauderdale Aquatic Center. Now we have over 250 swimmers, 22 practices a week to choose from, and the newly renovated, state-of-the-art, world class Fort Lauderdale Aquatic Center that is about to open.

I was a corporate human relations guy for years and left that to coach swimming. Now I have become a corporate human relations swimming coach.

Training Abbas was another challenge. I had a lot to learn. It was easy for my big extended family and swim family to adopt him immediately because he is very engaging. I hung on to the "this is just training another athlete" attitude. Through swimming, I have been to different countries all over the world so I knew something about different cultures. In this case, I had to add the current COVID-19 global pandemic; the City of Fort Lauderdale rules and restrictions in holding swim practices during COVID-19, the Tokyo Paralympics, and the refugee, immigration and UNHCR protocols, so this was going to be more complicated than just bettering the times on Abbas's 50-meter butterfly. I realized later that I would also be a language teacher and cultural advisor while watching closed captions during movies with him.

When Abbas first got here, I was overwhelmed. I thought my home would have to be ADA approved so I moved cabinets around. I hovered over him and assumed that I had to do everything. I had better open the door for him, how is he going to drink? I better have that filled water bottle ready, how is he going to open the refrigerator? On the first day I put the sliced turkey meat on the bottom shelf. The next morning when I woke up, he had made his own breakfast and opened up the cheese. After all of this time I can barely comprehend how he does everything without having arms. He is unbelievable.

The first time we went to the pool to meet the other coaches, Blake Woodrow, Mike Averett, and Ryan Rosenbaum, I did the same thing: Did he have his fins? Where should I put his water bottle? Was his backpack ready? Did he have a dry towel? After the first day, I was banned from being there and kicked off the deck by the other coaches. I wanted him to be as comfortable as possible so I emailed all the swimmers to make sure they knew about Abbas and sent them videos of him to watch.

I have been the coach of this team since 2004. I always have high expectations of my swimmers, and they know that I am not big on prima donnas and whiners. The team has strength and that was a good thing to offer him. The team exceeded my expectations and embraced Abbas as part of the team, and he soared to rock star status very quickly.

Abbas is a master at ingratiating himself. He had to use that skill to get the refugee camp staff to take him to swim practice since he couldn't go take a bus alone. He is a gifted diplomat who knows it and uses it to get what he wants. How do you turn a guy like this down? Swimming is about way more than swimming, and swimmers know this.

Abbas has some bad days. He gets cranky and tired just like the rest of us and that bad energy needs to go in the pool. I don't argue with him. Mike Ives would get angry with him, but I don't do that.

COVID-19 added another layer of complications because we had to wear a mask everywhere including swim practice. Like everyone else, COVID-19 severely limited my life and what I could do so it was good for me to have Abbas here and obsess about his needs. Restaurants were open for takeout only. I was cooking my own meals. Had it been two years earlier we would have gone out with other swimmers and social opportunities would be everywhere. I live walking-distance from lots of good restaurants and outdoor activities.

With the aquatic center still not completed, there were no 50-meter pools available to us, but we were grateful to have any pool to use since most swimmers all over the world had no pool at all.

Once we had these smaller, older pools to use, I had to figure out the logistics of how to get Abbas to and from those pools so he could swim when I was working. One of my swimmers is also my neighbor, and she offered to bring Abbas to practice. When I coached, he could come with me and sleep in the car or on the floor of my office. He is very structured in his routines and needs no prodding. Another swimmer, Debbie Rosenbaum, picked him up for practice and drove him home after and often they got bagels to eat after practice. Soon after, he got his own car, which was my old Mazda SUV, and he started driving himself to and from practice. A routine was falling into place for him.

For the most part Abbas and I are compatible. I get along with everyone and he made a conscious decision to be laser focused on Tokyo and the gold medal goal. He did not seek out the local Afghan diaspora community like he did in Portland because he thought that the Afghans would distract him. He also thought that being with Afghans would keep him from improving his English. He wanted to only live and breathe swimming."

THE SWIMMERS:

> AS MUCH AS I LOVE SWIMMING, SOMETIMES I WANT TO QUIT AND JUST GIVE IT UP. WHAT STOPS ME IS KNOWING THAT IF I DO THAT, I WOULD BE GIVING UP ON MYSELF. I CANNOT QUIT BECAUSE NO ONE WILL COME AND SAVE ME. I HAVE A POWERFUL AND DANGEROUS BRAIN. LIFE IS HARD AND YOU HAVE TO DEAL WITH THE UPS AND DOWNS. PEOPLE NEED TO MAKE THEIR OWN LIVES AND SOLVE THEIR PROBLEMS.

SOME PEOPLE CANNOT DO IT. I WAS LIKE THAT
TOO BUT I TRAINED MYSELF TO HAVE A STRONG
MIND AND RECOGNIZE WHAT IS WORTHWHILE.
PEOPLE DON'T WANT TO STRUGGLE AND FACE
CHALLENGES. I HAVE WORKED SO HARD TO GET
THIS STRENGTH.

I MUST PROTECT MY REPUTATION AND THE PEOPLE
WHO I LOOK UP TO AND WHO LOOK UP TO ME.
I CANNOT LET THEM DOWN AND I CANNOT LET
MYSELF DOWN. I HAVE TO KEEP MYSELF HAPPY.
THAT IS HOW A CHAMPION THINKS,
AND I AM A CHAMPION.

— ABBAS KARIMI —

WE SWIM WITH ABBAS AND THIS IS WHAT WE THINK

CLYDE AKBAR

I never thought that I would retire in Fort Lauderdale after all those years of freezing my ass off in Chicago. I have been on Swim Fort Lauderdale (SFTL) swim team for ten years, and I get up in the dark to swim. My doctor recommended swimming as my exercise for the injuries I got in Vietnam and Marty encouraged me to join the team. I am a Vietnam vet, and I have seen some tough guys in some tough situations. I cannot talk about Abbas without talking about Marty. If I could choose one guy to trust in the foxhole with me it would be Coach Marty.

In 2018, the Fort Lauderdale Aquatic Center pools closed for renovations. Marty found other pools for our team to swim in so that the team could stay together. Soon after came COVID-19, and Marty had to figure out how we could swim and stay safe. It was during this time Abbas came here to train with Marty for the Tokyo Paralympics and live in Marty's home. Marty embraced it all.

In 2022, the team is stronger than ever, and we keep winning. It is because of Marty. This is important so that you know what kind of person he is.

Here is my connection to Abbas: I was an immigrant from Trinidad 60 years ago and I am also Muslim, so Abbas and I share these things. Even though I lived in New York City and Chicago for many years I still have my Caribbean accent. I tried to get Abbas to come to my mosque but so far he has not.

I identify with Abbas. He is young and has a lot of changes yet to do. It will take a lot of patience. He has such lofty goals. He has to go through a lot of transitions. Here is what I tell him and other immigrants: Surround yourself with people who believe in you. Trust the people who care about you.

Here is how I made the adjustment for myself. I don't get involved and caught up with the different Muslim sects or the variety of ethnic groups here. We are just people with one creator. I adopted the attitude that I can relate to people everywhere. I feel at home everywhere. That is why I have the team spirit award. I hope that after Abbas returns from Afghanistan he comes to the Islamic Center of Broward mosque with me. There are all different sects there, there are women there, and I am the chef there.

Abbas became a US citizen in March of 2022, and we had a team party to celebrate that and some swimming accomplishments. Marty called me and asked me to give out the swimming awards and told me there was going to be a red white and blue cake with sparklers to celebrate Abbas. It was my special honor to play the *Star Spangled Banner* on my violin for Abbas at the party. I had no time to really practice so it was not my best performance because I had to read musical notes instead of playing from my heart. I had four T-shirts made for Abbas with the American flag on it and the United States on it. He wore those for days. There were a lot of teared up eyes at that party.

Abbas and I have discussed his intended visit to Afghanistan to see his mother and the rest of his family. He knows that I'm concerned for his safe return to the U.S.

I have shared with Abbas that descendant groups in Kabul have no power over faith in God. For Abbas to accomplish the high goals he has set for himself, he will need patience, and to identify those who have his best interest at heart. This will take time. It's a process.

I told Abbas that I had to come to peace with myself. The Taliban is feared all over the world, but they are weak with their influence with God. If God wants him to return, he will return. He will grow his beard, he will not go to certain dangerous places. He is an American now with an American passport. He can be more reserved and quiet, but word will travel fast that he has returned. Mohammadi has assured him that he will be safe. Abbas wants to remain low key, but they will know he is there when he shows up at the pool to swim.

He has to be careful for himself and for his mother. She would never forgive herself if something happens to him.

During the months that he returns to Kabul, he will realize that he doesn't really fit in there anymore. When he is here, he will realize he is still outside of the mainstream here too. He is an in-between person, just like I was and just like so many people here are.

Abbas brings his uniqueness to the team. At swim meets, the place is on fire when he is swimming with the entire team proudly cheering for him. The other teams are just dazzled, and his international status gives prestige to our team. He belongs and is an important part of who we are.

He will eventually go to Colorado Springs to train, but when he comes back he will always be part of Swim Fort Lauderdale.

CHRIS M^cPHERSON
HEAD COACH, ENSWORTH AQUATICS MASTERS SWIMMING, NASHVILLE, TENNESSEE

I really didn't know Abbas when he came with Marty to visit me in Nashville. Marty and I are both USMS masters coaches and we grew up in the same area of Maryland near Washington, DC. We both swam as kids, know a lot of the same people, and he was a mentor to me as a coach. We are close personal friends. It was the middle of the pandemic and Abbas needed to swim some long course practices since there were no long course pools available to him in Fort Lauderdale. It was a chance for Marty to get another set of eyes on Abbas's swimming before the Tokyo Paralympics. My specialty is technique, and I am glad I got to work with him. We also did a lot of work on the starting blocks.

Marty didn't think there was a problem with Abbas's stroke; he just wanted him to be faster. We adjusted his kick and body position making sure that he leaned forward and took quicker breaths. He was doing wide kicks, and we adjusted those to be tighter, stronger kicks where he is using his core instead of his thighs.

For his starts, we worked on his springing off the starting block. The steps are placing your feet with one foot forward and one back, with the heel at the back of the block. Then you bend your knees and get comfortable. The next part is to lean down and get your rear end up and lean forward. By positioning like this, the swimmer is primed to do underwater kicking. For Abbas, he has to get the thrust from his chest because he does not have arms.

He got faster on the block and in the water. His body was more engaged, and he felt better.

The second time he came to Nashville, we worked with orthopedic trainer Jasper Richardson who has worked with Olympic athletes. My concern is that Abbas does a lot of dryland training on his own, and I wanted to make sure that he was doing it properly. I had good resources, and I was glad to use them.

Before Abbas got here, I was concerned about him accepting me as a coach since I knew that Afghan men did not perceive women in a position of authority. We totally bonded, went out to dinner, and he stayed at my house. We went running together and he was open and respectful. He fell in love with my dogs and I saw him be totally relaxed. Abbas is so serious about swimming.

He fit in well with my Ensworth swimmers and also talked to the age group swimmers.

While he and Marty were here, Abbas was studying for the U.S. citizenship test.

During his stay, he would get up at 3 a.m., pray, then eat oatmeal and have coffee. He forgot to pack his bowl and mug, but he adapted and figured out how to use what I had.

I was honored that they came to visit and trusted me with the training. I felt like a surrogate mother.

I met Abbas' whole family on the computer. His family found a wife for him, although he has never met her in person. During his stay, Khaled Hosseini interviewed Abbas for the UNHCR.

Remember when Marty said that during the Tokyo competition he was texting with someone when things turned bad? That was me.

HOW I DO IT: MY WORKOUT AND STRETCHING, EATING, AND SLEEPING

I have been stretching since I was 12 and I never miss a day. I learned the stretching routine from kickboxing, a lot of it is like yoga. Stretching keeps my legs flexible, so it makes reaching high places with my feet easier, and I can be comfortable when I drive. When driving, I keep my left foot on the steering wheel and my right foot on the gas and brake. Since I get up around 3:30 a.m., I go to 5:30 a.m. practice and drive myself there. I used to go with Marty, but now I have my own car and I just meet him there.

Before I stretch, I warm up by running. Sometimes it is a distance run for about a half hour, other times it is a series of sprints. This warmup is good for my swimming.

I wear headphones the entire time and listen to Afghan country music. It makes me feel happy, confident, and focused. Stretching is also very calming, and I always feel very good after I do it.

I do each exercise a few times for 2-3 minutes. The stretches are done very gradually to keep me from pulling muscles. The circuit takes me about a half hour, and I do them every day. You must start a routine like this very slowly. I have added the bridges and the Russian twists for my abdominal muscles. Abs are so important because they keep your back strong.

It is important to know this: Swimming is basically the physics of how the body can efficiently cut through water. The more efficient the body can propel itself, the faster the body can go. The body is propelled when the limbs and the torso are coordinated in repeated motion and rely on the body's natural buoyancy. Disabled swimmers have to adapt. Since 2010, the Americans with Disabilities Act has required that swimming pools in the United States be accessible to disabled swimmers. It is not like this in Afghanistan and in many other countries.

I swim six days a week for one hour. Some days I swim a double practice. I don't ever swim alone, always with the team. Because our team is so big, I have to always share a lane with someone. Even with no arms I am often the fastest swimmer on the team.

WEIGHTS

At first I trained on my own. Lots of the martial arts training translates to swimming. When Coach Nick from the USA Paralympic team altered my weights program, I followed that. I do mostly core workouts that my local trainer has incorporated for me. The repetitions have increased. I have gotten less aggressive with weights because I injured my knees.

I do dryland three times a week and one of those times I do it on my own.

STRETCHING

Stretching keeps my legs flexible so that I can reach high places and eat and drink comfortably. First I run 20 to 30 minutes, sometimes I run sprints to get warmed up. I run to the beach and walk back. After that I start stretching.

These are my stretches:

180-degree stretch.

Butterfly stretch.

Standing 180-degree stretch.

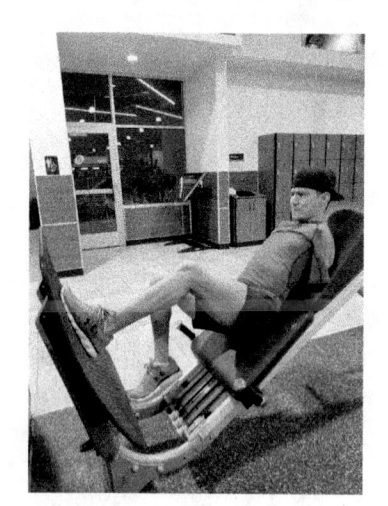

In the gym.

I hold my stretches for 2 to 3 minutes

The pigeon is a gradual stretch but a really good one. I am used to doing these stretches but my body must be warmed up. I spend a half hour every day stretching before swimming. It keeps me motivated and it makes it possible to have my legs also function as arms.

When I swim, I breathe on my left side only.

EATING AND DIET

I eat bread for all three meals and sometimes I have cheese. I eat pasta or rice, chicken, beef, turkey, and any kind of fresh vegetables and fresh fruits. I eat potatoes too. For a treat, I might have cheesecake but no sauces. Salmon, eggs, fish, and lamb are my proteins. I eat yogurt but no sour cream. I opt for whole grain breads and, occasionally, ice cream or a cookie.

Eating like this gives me an energy boost. Clean eating is what I follow and that means no pizza, no lasagna, no greasy or fried food, no spices, and no salt. I am even starting to not like bad food anymore because I associate it with poor performance.

I don't eat anything with tomatoes or made from tomatoes like ketchup because it does not agree with me. Eating like this gives me more energy in swimming but it will take a long time to get faster. It is like getting good gasoline in the car. The wrong gas makes a car run poorly. My training includes making these food choices a number one priority. Rest counts too, but it's all connected. I like so many different kinds of food. All of these things have to be in sync.

I can relax my food choices when I am not training for an important swim meet. My relaxed food choices include hamburgers, burritos, and orange chicken. The hamburgers in the United States are so delicious. I had them in Kabul but they are different here.

SLEEP

I go to sleep early every day, and I also nap very deeply for one to three hours every day after I watch a movie.

MY ROUTINE

Pray

Swim

Eat

Pray

Watch TV, one movie a day

Pray/Sleep

Three times a week: dry land training for 2 hours

I speak to family members at 4 a.m.

HEADPHONES

I had small headphones when I left Afghanistan but now I have Beats that cover my ears. I listen to Afghan country music when I train, and this is a way for me to escape and be in my own world. I got them in Portland. I feel focused and happy when I train with my music from home.

MY THOUGHTS

I see myself as the winner. I think positive thoughts. I am human so sometimes I slip, but being positive helps with everything. I constantly think about swimming and training, and often I swim a race in my head while I am doing something else.

I missed qualifying for the World Paralympic Championship in Manchester, England, in August of 2023, by 2 seconds. I am good for a relay because I am the only S5 butterfly swimmer, but Leanne, our freestyler, has a problem with her eye so there is no relay I can be in. The next meet is in Santiago, Chile.

MY LOVE LIFE BEFORE I MET MY WIFE, ZAINAB

I am 25 now and that is considered old to not be married. I will be 27 on January 1, 2024. My brothers married at 22 and 23, and I feel pressure to have someone in my life. I am certain that I need a woman from my own culture. Most Afghan marriages are arranged, and half of the brides are under 16. The average age for boys is 18. Marrying relatives within the family is often encouraged, it keeps families connected, and it limits outsiders from diluting the family and is known as *endogamous*. My family has married this way, and I am going to do that too.

I see my role like my father's role was: in total control. I am responsible for giving a woman money, a house, and helping her with things she cannot do. However, I am the boss, I make the decisions, and my wife must be there for me and respect me at all times. I am responsible for taking her 'to heaven.'

> **People in the United States always tell me that I don't need a wife, I just need sex. In my culture, we don't have sex without marriage. I don't fit into this part of American society. It is**

too aggressive for me. Yet, the touch of a woman electrifies me. Even when I was getting my teeth cleaned the hygienist put her hand on my cheek and I felt something.
It is not easy to find a girl here who is not a drinker, and I don't want to drink. I still cannot get used to how the girls here basically wear their panites and bras at the beach. It is exciting, but mostly, it makes me uncomfortable.

I have many women in my life now, Andrea and my training partner in the gym are both women, and we have shared meals together.

I could have a lot of girlfriends. Women are attracted to me. I am different in culture, in looks, in the way I talk, in my outlook on life, in my unique past, and I am passionate about what I want to do. Arms don't matter. Confidence matters. Passion matters.
After all of these years, what once repelled girls now attracts them.
As difficult as it is for me to maneuver without arms, I knew that if I had them then I would be like everybody else. My disability makes me special.
I was hungry for attention even as a little kid and I especially wanted the girls to pay attention to me so I always tried to look the best I could.
Girls did not give a shit about me, and that rejection has contributed to my ability to have a cold heart all these years later. As quickly as I connect and attach to people, there is a huge part of me that is very cold, and I know that it comes from this. I pay close attention to how women treat me and am very careful because some of them just want to use me, for money, for citizenship, for the shine I bring on myself that they could be part of. It is not easy for me to trust them. Women paid attention to me once I began to succeed as a swimmer. They are attracted to my success and drive,

my relentlessness, and that I can do something other people cannot. Without arms I am unique and powerful.
Since I have been in Fort Lauderdale, I have communicated with Afghan women online, none of whom were right for me.

Shokoria

My family found Shokoria for me while they were in Pakistan, but she was not a good match. She was not interested in my life, only what I could provide for her. I never met her in person and never will. I wanted to show her, on my phone, what Fort Lauderdale looks like. She did not care at all and that told me a lot.

Pari

Pari helped me deal with my breakup with Shokoria and then she and I started talking, and we evolved into a three month online romance. I learned a lot about myself and what is right for me. Pari had goals of being a nurse and a boxer, neither of which women are allowed to do in Afghanistan. I helped her and her family get to Pakistan where she could pursue those goals. We had the athlete mentality in common, but it fell apart when her mother thought that I supported my family too much and would not be able to take care of her.

Like Shokoria, I never met Pari in person either. It was more of an emotional breakup, but I was solid in my decision. I also was solid about this: I need my family to find me a traditional Hazara woman who will support my goals and do what I want. A wife is family and she must fit into my family.

CAUTION: GIRLS WILL TRY TO USE ME

For example, an Afghan girl living in Miami showed an interest in me. She had lost part of her arm in an accident, and she reached out to me since we shared a similar handicap. We met for dinner in Aventura, about 30 minutes south of where I live in Fort Lauderdale. She was ten years older than I was, wore lots of makeup, and clothes that were too tight.

We spoke Dari during dinner. She seemed to really like me, and we made plans to see each other again. The next time I saw her, she offered me $20,000 to get her citizenship. That pissed me off. She was just looking for someone to do this for her. Besides, how dare she offer me that amount of money! If I were selling citizenship, I could get $100,000.

Those women took up a lot of my time, and I am reminded to focus on my real true love who is always there for me, who never disappoints me: who is beautiful, predictable, and loyal: Swimming.

THIRTEEN
I NEED TO GO HOME

If you go anywhere, even paradise, you will miss your home.

— Malala Yousafzai —

Pakistani Nobel Prize-winning human rights advocate, especially the education of women and children.

Abbas in traditional Afghan clothes.

I have lost interest in becoming a champion. Swimming is not making me happy right now because I need to go home and see my family. Maybe I will come back alive and maybe I won't, but I don't want to regret not going there, and I would. I want to see my mother, and I will always regret not seeing my father before he died.

> ***I dream about going to Kabul and being the little boy on my mother's lap and crying for all the years it took for me to get here. With my American passport I can visit whenever I want.***

I had to wait to go on this trip because there was a mistake on my passport that had to be fixed. Somehow it said that I was female, something I assure you I am not. Mohammadi promised me that once I got there that I would be safe. We are going to visit Karizak, my father's village in the country with a river that you can drink from. It is so quiet there, and my father's grave is there.

I am taking lots of luggage with shoes, t-shirts, my swimming medals; plus I am taking goggles, caps, shirts, towels, and swim equipment for Afghan swimmers.

I have a one-way ticket, and I don't know when I'm coming back.

COACH MARTY HENDRICK

A GOOD LEADER INSPIRES PEOPLE TO HAVE CONFIDENCE IN THE LEADER. A GREAT LEADER INSPIRES PEOPLE TO HAVE CONFIDENCE IN THEMSELVES.

— Eleanor Roosevelt —

I am concerned that Abbas has lost focus. He came to me in 2020 with a solid goal of a gold medal, totally focused. He got his citizenship, and he made the refugee Paralympic team. Now family is his focus. He wants them to find him a wife. He talks about World's in Manchester, England, in August of 2023, but not the 2024 Paralympics games in Paris.

I am concerned for his safety when he goes back to Kabul. He can get locked up, they can take his passport, he could disappear, and the United States cannot help him. He will get no money from the United States.

For an hour a day, he and I still laugh and smile, but he just wants to go home.

I told him, you live in the United States now, you can have your own culture, but it is totally different from American culture, and you cannot expect Americans to adapt to your culture. Sometimes I joke with him and call him Taliban.

I have faith in Abbas. Why would I doubt him? He succeeds at every impossible thing he does.

ABBAS GOES HOME TO KABUL

I had a 15-hour, 15-minute flight on Emirates from Miami to Dubai. My plan is to stay in Dubai for a few days with some friends, adjust to the time change, then take a three hour flight to Kabul.

I flew on Emirates flight 214 from Miami to Dubai (213 is the return). The beautiful flight attendants were so nice to me and helped me out by making sure that I was comfortable and had a lot of space to eat. There were lots of good movies to watch. I saw *Samaritan*, *Top Gun*, and *Super-Pets*. I bought my ticket with some of the money I earned from breaking a world record and getting a gold medal in the Portugal meet.

All I could think about was spending time with my family and the marriage they were arranging for me.

In Dubai I stayed with my brother and sister who live in Sharjah, a half-hour outside of Dubai. I met a nephew for the first time and spent time seeing beautiful Dubai and eating great food.

I also went to Abu Dhabi, 87 miles away. We visited the Sheik Zayed Grand Mosque, and I went to pray there. This huge mosque has the world's largest prayer carpet that was hand knotted by 1,300 Iranian artists. The mosque is full of one-of-a-kind treasures like gold-plated Swarovski chandeliers, vast marble mosaics, and reflective pools with amethyst- and jasper- embedded columns.

Because the United Arab Emirates is a Muslim country I heard the *Adhan*, the call to prayer, something I had not heard in ten years. Its familiarity from my childhood gave me peace. The word *Adhan* means announcement. It can be heard up to five times a day in Muslim communities, once for each of the five daily prayers.

The Islamic call to prayer is not only a way to express Islamic faith. It is also the way for a Muslim community to declare its presence in a country.

Abu Dhabi seems like a good place to live for families, but you will always be a resident, never a citizen. I thought a lot about my future during this visit and what I am going to do after I finish competing in swimming. Maybe I could sell cars and engines like my brother and father. For the first time, I felt relaxed, no anxiety or depression. I spent time shopping and bought gold earrings and a locket for both my fiancé and some for Asghar's fiancé too.

ARRIVING IN KABUL

It is a three-hour flight from Dubai to Kabul. The Taliban are the first people you see at the Hamid Karzai Kabul airport. They are in charge of the country, and I just have to go along with them. They respect athletes and now that I am famous, they will protect me. One of my Afghan friends in Portland just visited Kabul, and he said it was fine.

Returning to Kabul is the right thing for me to do.

I plan to swim in the new pool that my brother built and also swim at Lajward pool where swimming first started for me. Once I start to swim people will know I am there. I'm a well-known legend at home.

I believe things in Afghanistan will get better for women, but for now, they cannot do much other than wear a burqa, stay home, raise kids, cook, and take care of husbands.

My plan is to not make waves, not give opinions, just go along and stay out of the spotlight. I will wear Afghan-style clothes, loose pants, a beard, long tunics, no tight jeans and tshirts. The *perahan tunban* is the standard traditional uniform dress for men, consisting of a tunic shirt that covers the knee, a vest, pants, and with (optional) head covering. A thick shawl called *patu* can be worn in the winter. This dress originates from the Pashtun lands but its use spreads to most of Afghanistan. It remains the predominant dress for male villagers.

I will fit in and be calm.

The Beast will be under control.

My family has always been there for me, and I will not be at peace until I am with them once again. I love Afghanistan, but I had to leave it. It was always my plan to return and see everyone, and once I do that, my swim goals will be refreshed. This trip is going to propel me, but like always, people doubt me.

Mohammadi helped me plan my trip home. He says the Taliban will treat me special. I think that people there must go along with them for now or fight to change it.

If I die on this trip, I have no regrets. If I did not go then I would not be a good person. I am going back as the loving person I have always been.

It will be nice when I eventually leave Kabul to take an airplane this time instead of being smuggled in the back of a truck under a blue tarp.

Mohammadi, his kids, Asghar, my mom, and my sister all came to get me at the airport. Mohammadi drove his Toyota and the brakes were not working very well. This was the first time I saw the Taliban. They were on the streets carrying guns. Everything here looked worn out to me, the buildings, the people, the streets. I wanted to see all the Pashtun people. They are descendants of Alexander the Great, who invaded the area in B.C.E. 330. Most of them today are Sunni Muslims, although a few are Shiite like I am. Former Afghan president Hamid Karzai, and 2014 Nobel Peace Prize laureate Malala Yousafzai are Pashtun.

…I started to cry when I saw my family…I couldn't talk…I just cried and cried…I saw them on the phone all the time but this was different—I was overwhelmed with emotion.

KABUL

Asghar's girlfriend Eda is going to be his wife. She came from Turkey through Iran by herself and stayed there with one of my sisters for a few days.

While I was in Kabul I bought a white 2000 Lexus SUV. The Taliban stopped me at the checkpoints at first and asked me why I was driving with my feet. Then they saw that I had no arms, and they were impressed with how I drove the car. They asked me a lot of questions, searched the car, and let me go. My family has the car now although they don't drive it much because fuel is so expensive, the same price as fuel in Fort Lauderdale.

At first I was afraid when the Taliban stopped me at a checkpoint. They can stop you at any time and check your car, remove you from your car, check your pockets. They look for guns, they look for drugs or for anything that could be used as a weapon. Arbitrary checkpoints are everywhere, and if you are caught with these things they will beat you, take your car, and put you in prison. They can do anything that they want to you. Trafficking drugs is big business here, and the Taliban wants to be in control of it. They will smoke weed and do what they want because they are in power. I try to see them as people doing a job, they have the big guns, the uniforms, they are the soldiers in charge of the country.

They were nice to me and impressed with my car. Having a driver's license and car insurance is more of a suggestion than a law here. If you get in an accident then you pay to fix it or lose your car. When I first came to the United States I was amazed at all the rules about what you need to live your life, let alone drive your car.

I felt respected, and I passed all the checkpoints after I told them I was a swimmer, and they invited me to get a medal. I rejected their invitation and they did not force me. I did not get their medal because I am an American and I do not want to advertise myself. I want to keep myself private and under the radar. I often thought that if the Taliban makes me their king then I could make Afghanistan a better place. I did not get involved with their politics. In reality, they don't care about me. I am not a big deal. I acted confident and brave. They left me alone and I stopped being afraid of them.

Anything can happen, and people here generally feel uneasy and afraid so they just obey the rules. I don't want to talk bad about the Taliban, they did not give me any trouble. I don't really give a shit about them. People here are starving, not just poor people, rich people are in trouble too. It is very simple: you need to be quiet about what you have, and you need to not steal from others, tempting as it may be. If the Taliban catches thieves, they will send them to prison. If they resist and fight back, they will kill them.

Still, as confident as I was about staying safe, I was not comfortable going outside. I was born here, I grew up with edginess like this, this is how it is here. I had to face my fear and go out anyway. It is always a little scary, but it is natural for me. I knew that a bomb could explode or that I could get kidnapped.

This is not paranoia that would make me think that. Shortly after I got here, there was a suicide attack inside the Kaaj Educational Center where 35 Hazara girls were killed and over 80 others were injured. ISIS-K and Taliban are the suspects. There have been decades of persecution of the Hazara tribe, and since the Taliban takeover it has increased, and this attack was related to that. There are also reports of arbitrary arrests, torture, and other ill treatment as well as inflammatory speech on line and in some mosques calling for Hazaras to be killed. The Kaaj Center is about 200 meters from my house. This happened on a Friday morning. I was at the cemetery, but the rest of my family heard it. I was surprised but I wasn't.

Kabul looks familiar to me but worn out and everywhere there are so many poor people. My family would be poor, too, if I didn't support them. They have enough food because of me. I suppose some of the Afghans might not like that I have become an American citizen, but for the most part, people here have too much of their own lives to worry about to be concerned with what I do.

BAND E AMIR AGAIN

During my visit, I went back to Band E Amir with my brothers, nephews, and some friends too. We drove my new Lexus there, about a 10-hour drive on both a concrete road then a dirt road, which is why it takes a long time to get there. We stopped on the way to get water and food, then spent the night with a family friend who lives near Band E Amir

The water at Band E Amir felt like ice water when I jumped in and swam 100 meters for everyone. It is so quiet there. This was the first time any of them saw me swim other than in videos. No women were there because they are not allowed to visit unless they are with a man.

> *I promised myself that I would come back to Band E Amir. This is still considered holy water and although my arms never grew, I like to think that the water there gave me the magical power to swim. People there never saw anyone like me swim. All you could hear was the sound of my swimming, nothing else.*
>
> *The water is a scary dark, vibrant blue, and you cannot see the bottom. There is nothing else in the whole world like these seven lakes that make up Band E Amir.*

While I was in Kabul, I saw Qasim, the lifeguard who taught me to swim. We were happy to see each other, and we have been in touch all along, especially when he needs me. He uses me for what he needs, and I appreciate all he has done for me. He and I have an understanding: We care deeply about each other, and it has evolved into a business arrangement.

I didn't swim much while I was in Kabul. I was so busy with my family. Maybe I swam twice a week, but I was not motivated to swim more than that. Swimming is never easy, and during this time it almost defeated me.

MEETING MY WIFE, ZAINAB

My arranged marriage with Mayria, a pretty, 17-year-old, did not happen. She did not want to go ahead with our arranged marriage, and she had met someone else.

Since I no longer had a fianceé, I became interested in 19-year-old Zainab, my first cousin who I have known since she was a baby. Her mother is my father's sister. You can marry your first cousin in Afghanistan, and actually, it is encouraged. After I expressed interest in her, my family asked her family if she was interested in me. Both families thought the marriage was a good choice. Zainab and I have a lot in common, and we are both Shiite Muslim. I was glad that she accepted me.

It is better for me to have a girl that was chosen for me, American girls are too different for me, even Muslim-American girls.

I spent three weeks getting to know Zainab. During our time together we planned the wedding, went shopping together, and got our clothes for the wedding. I gave up on all other women after I met her. She is soft and kind and has a pure heart. I get emotional thinking about her.

I took Zainab to Karizak, my father's village, about a five-hour drive from Kabul. Mohammadi drove my car while she fed me grapes. She is very nice to me, quiet and shy. She likes chocolate and is very tiny and so pretty. At first she just listened to me. In Karizak there is a river to drink from, and she held the water bottle for me to drink from. I used to come here as a boy, and now I am here with my future wife. My father's grave is here, and this was the first time I saw it. I cried while I was there for all the time it took me to come back here.

Her mother, who is also my aunt, is so happy about us.

During this trip, Zainab learned about my life, and eventually she became more comfortable with me. We sat by the river and talked so much and learned about each other.

Zainab also met The Beast.

The Beast reared its ugly head with her because she is young and childish so my tolerance for her immaturity got short. Living alone for ten years matured me, and I don't have a lot of patience for immaturity. I still have some hate inside of me, I have shitty things inside of me and that is part of who I am.

I talked a lot to my father at his grave and updated him on my life.

GETTING MARRIED

It was time to get married. I took Zainab to buy clothes for both the wedding and for Kina Gecesi, also known as henna night. For this we got dressed up in green and me and Asghar wore traditional Afghan clothes.

Kina Gecesi is a women's party before marriage that includes eating, singing, and acknowledging the sadness of leaving your mother. Henna night has been a Turkish tradition for hundreds of years. A day or two before the wedding, families and friends gather for this small celebration. Traditional folk songs are sung, and henna is applied on the bride's palm and the groom's pinky finger and in my case on my middle toe.

Our wedding was very early in the morning at the Qasre Mahtab Wedding Hall in Kabul. We had a double wedding with Asghar and Eda. The women got professional makeup, and everyone wore white. There are no pictures of the brides to show because women are kept private and belong only to their husbands and family.

The ceremony and the party were so much fun although it all went so fast. I couldn't fully relax because I was worried there would be explosions. I prayed that this day would be safe.

I was excited to be with Zainab, although she was scared and nervous. We had nearly 2000 people at the wedding, many members of the Hazara tribe, extended family, people who I grew up with, neighbors, people from the mosque, people our family has done business with. We hosted lunch with assorted meats, chicken, lamb, and beef.

It made me realize that Kabul is my home no matter what.

The house that I grew up in needed repair. Before the wedding we put flowers all over and made our bedroom as pretty as we could. I put lights in there, and it looked nice. It was our room for the three months that I was there. My mother got her wish by seeing us married. Her next wish is for us to have a baby but I don't want our baby to be born in Kabul, which would be so hard for me.

During these three months, the whole family ate meals together. Mohammadi's wife cooked the food, and everyone cleaned up. Zainab can shop or go to a restaurant but she cannot go outside unless she has permission from me or my brothers or it could be trouble from the Taliban. She cannot communicate with other men, and since I am gone, Mohammadi is in charge of the whole family.

I miss Zainab. We hugged at night and she would scratch my ear. I would wake up with her. I wanted so much to do this, and it was everything I thought it would be.

I want to eventually bring her to the United States. To do so, I have to fill out paperwork, get a lawyer, and get a sponsor. It will take a long time to get her here. I plan to go back to Kabul before the 2024 Paralympics, but for now, I will talk to her every day and call her at 4 a.m. She texts me, leaves voice messages. I am lonely without her and I feel better when I talk to her. I also call my brother, sister, and mother, but first I call Zainab. She has an Afghanistan passport so she can go to other countries, but I have to make a good income to support her and that will take at least a year. Whatever is best for me is when I will say when she can come. It cannot happen right away. She would have to get a visa. I don't want to leave her alone there. I want to bring her here and have her by my side. It is scary to think about her without me. All of this is another huge challenge, but like with all the other things, I will make this happen too. For now there is comfort knowing that she is with my family.

It was hard to leave everyone and come back to Fort Lauderdale, but what soothes me is knowing that now I can come back and visit again because I am an American citizen with a USA passport.

MY TRIP BACK TO FORT LAUDERDALE

As hard as it was to leave my wife and my family, I am happy to be back in Fort Lauderdale, back to my goal and back to the pool. I missed the beauty and calmness here. Swimming is my one shot at the life I want. I have to take control of my future, and marriage made me want to do this.

I need new sponsors. I am one second away from qualifying time to be part of the USA Paralympic National team. My Airbnb sponsorship is over, but Arena has remained my sponser. Toyota is a possibility after I am a member of the USA Paralympic team. I am ready to train again, the fire to win is in me again. I need money, I may have to just get a regular job.

In October of 2022, after nearly four years of construction, the Fort Lauderdale Aquatic Center opened and now I have a state-of-the-art 50-meter long course pool to train in. I have been in pools all over the world, and this one is the best, but I am not emotionally attached to it like the other swimmers are. It is just another pool for me. I did not get to use this pool when I needed it. Even when it was ready, the city would not let me use it. I am actually more attached to the older smaller pool at Carter Park. It feels like home, and I love it there.

WHY I AM SPECIAL: THIS IS MY MANTRA, THIS IS WHAT I REMIND MYSELF. I MUST ALWAYS REMEMBER THIS:

I am known all over the world in the swimming community.

Because of this book, because of the media attention on me, because of the documentary being made about my life, everyone will know about me.

I was able to leave Kabul and become a U.S. citizen.

I have seen a good portion of the world.

I can speak 4 languages: Dari, Farsi, Turkish, and English.

I have propelled past my disability.

I have a wife now and a future with her.

I am an inspiration to other swimmers and other Paralympic athletes.

I am a voice for refugees, over 117 million of them through the UNHCR.

I have something special to offer.

I have friends from all over the world.

I have an explosive social media presence.

I have The Beast under control…well, sort of.

I have learned to control my body, and be in the best physically fit shape possible.

I have a unique confidence that propels me in to any kind of audience or social situation.

My shot for a successful life is through swimming…

This quote by Israelmore Ayivor really sums up my life story:

> PEOPLE WHO SWIM VERY WELL IN TROUBLED WATERS ARE MORE RESPECTED AND CELEBRATED THAN THOSE WHO SWIM EXCELLENTLY IN CALM WATERS.
>
> — ISRAELMORE AYIVOR —

FULL CIRCLE

I am blessed to have made our mother (and father) so proud. Mohammadi, his wife and his five children arrived in Fort Lauderdale on May 12, 2023. All my life he supported me, he helped me with crucial decisions in my life: Do I leave Afghanistan, do I stay in Turkey, do I pursue swimming, do I get married. I look to him for guidance and he is always there. As complicated as it was for me to get to where I am, it was also very difficult for Mohammadi and his family to come here. They had to buy Turkish citizenships for seven people, then fly from Istanbul to Brazil. From there, they came to the Mexican border and were smuggled into California. Then they flew from San Diego to Fort Lauderdale, and are renting a temporary home. They don't have jobs, money, or a permanent place to stay yet. Mohammadi just got his international driver's license. With his skill set and relentless drive, he will succeed.

He disobeyed our father to support my dream. Now I am helping him get settled here, and I will do whatever it takes.

> ONCE YOU BECOME FEARLESS,
> LIFE BECOMES LIMITLESS.

EPILOGUE

My close family is now spread out, Alem and his family remain in Kabul, Zainab, my mother, Asghar, and Eda are with my sister in Mashhad, Iran, Mohammadi and his family arrived in Fort Lauderdale on May 13, 2023. The story of how they got here is worthy of its own separate book. Getting out of Afghanistan was not easy for them. At the checkpoints, they were asked a lot of questions about why they were flying to Tehran, and they said they were simply going to visit my sister.

Mohammadi could only afford to bring his own immediate family to the United States. He had to sell his 2010 Land Cruiser so that he had the money to go. He also has a part ownership in a pool/sauna/spa, and he had to get the money out of that. He, his wife, and their five children left Fort Lauderdale after two months and are now resettled in an Afghan community in Edmonton, Alberta.

* Alem's daughter is engaged to Mohammadi's son. They are 14 years old, and this is a safe way to keep cohesiveness within the family.

*Documentary – The University of Miami Cinematic Arts department is making a documentary film about me. They are currently filming the trailer. I always wanted to be an actor in a movie but I never imagined there would be a movie about me. They have come to my swim practices and filmed me with drones. They are going to film a day-in-my-life video too, to see how I do everything. Once they have a trailer, they will sell it to a streaming service or a film festival.

*Minneapolis –…I won a silver medal for the back stroke and a gold for the 50-meter butterfly (.37). I also had the documentary film crew there. At first that was distracting but then I didn't care. We got to be friends and now it will be easier to have them around. I also got to know my teammates better on this trip. Although I got the medals, my times (.37 for the 50-meter butterfly) were a second short of qualifying time to be a full-time USA Paralympic team member. I came back to Fort Lauderdale pissed at swimming and pissed at myself.

I am famous now and have a social media following from all around the world. Afghans are angry that I am an American, and I have a lot of haters because of that.

* The Feb 18/19, 2023–Masters Challenge meet: I swam the 50-meter butterfly in .31, my fastest time ever.

* September 2023–For a second time as an American citizen, I went to Kabul to visit my family.

* November 2023–I am swimming in the Pan American Games in Santiago Chile–a measuring tool for the journey to the Paris Paralympics. It is a colorful high-profile meet.

* I am now a client of CG Sports Management, a comprehensive sports management company.

* Coach Marty Hendrick has been selected as a USA paralympic coach for the PanAmerican Games in Santiago, Chile. I was selected to represent Team USA in this meet and will be swimming in four events: 50 Fly, 50 Back, 50 and 100 Free.

* Through CG Sports Management, I have my own website: Abbas-Karimi.com

* November 2023–I spoke to three groups of students at Florida State University where I told them my life story. This was my first time as a paid speaker.

*I got two bronze medals at the Santiago Para Pan American Games.

At the swim meet they say, "In lane 4, from the United States of America...Abbas Karimi..." it is still amazing to be introduced that way, as an American...

I have friends in Turkey and Iran plus coaches and teammates that cared about me in Portland.

I had to leave them all to follow my dream. I have to keep leaving people behind, people I love.

It hits me hard sometimes. The people in my life are content with doing the same things all the time but that is not me. I have to keep changing and growing.

I am still not good at being told what to do, that has never changed.

Swimming helps calm me down and if I keep swimming then I have consistency. It gives me a focus in my life, something to be king of. I want to be so big but I know that in success you fail over and over. I am tough and I do not give up. When doors slam at me I get stronger. I missed important competitions during my peak years because of not being a Turkish citizen. I missed training because of COVID-19. Sometimes I am both proud of myself and angry at myself at the same time. I talk to myself in English so that I become better and better at it.

I am a married man now. I still want more. I still need to focus more. I need to be bigger, I need to keep swimming, and I need to have one focus only: Paris, 2024.

When I die, I want people to know that I, Abbas Karimi, without arms, never gave up on my dreams and my goals. I can do something to change the world and I can do that by being a champion, a Paralympic champion.

— Abbas's sporting philosophy, May 12, 2021 —

AFTERWORD

How I met Abbas and how this book came to be.

Anita Mitchell

Anita and Abbas.

Like the rest of our team of over 250 swimmers, I was excited to meet Abbas. In the video, he swam like an ultra-fast snake. As a former television news producer assignment editor, I recognized his story as a great one. A world-champion swimmer without arms who left Afghanistan and was smuggled through Iran into Turkey and eventually made it to Fort Lauderdale? It doesn't get much better than that.

It was easy to spot Abbas on his first day of practice. I missed the first 50 meters of my own warmup so that I could watch his.

He immediately earned respect from his new team. We admire each other's swimming. Swimmers form a kinship right away, because we already have so much in common. We get dressed in cars, shower with hoses, eat voraciously after swimming, and become addicted to the peace we feel after a workout.

About a year later, Marty told me that a literary agent was looking for a ghostwriter to help tell Abbas's story. Would I be interested? He told me to think about it during practice.

I had recently retired as a writer. I had just recovered from an illness. I was seventy-one. I knew all too well how much work this would be. Do I need this? Do I want to put the rest of my life on pause to pursue this? Is this an important story that will inspire others? Am I the right person for this project?

By the time I was finishing my last 100 meters, I knew it would be an honor for me to do this.

Abbas's life story touches every possible human condition.

During my twenty-six years as a breaking news editor and field producer at local Miami FOX television affiliate WSVN-7, I wrote about murders, court cases, freeway car pile-ups, sex assaults, cars crashing into buildings, cars diving into canals, alligators where they are not supposed to be, people where they are not supposed to be, injustices galore, politics ad nauseam—all of it on deadline.

I always knew that those years were really my training for something else. Writing this book is that something else.

Marty Hendrick, Abbas's coach, has been my coach for twenty years. Under his tutelage, I have earned national championship medals for freestyle, backstroke, breaststroke, butterfly, and relays; I also gained world recognition for a relay. I understand the rules of competition and what it takes to be an athlete, whether a fitness swimmer (like me) or an elite athlete like Abbas. We often refer to our swim practices as our special version of a submerged martini. Like Abbas, I will continue to swim as long as my body can do it.

After I met Abbas, I contacted Brian Entin, from WGN NewsNation, and producer Daniel Cohen, from WSVN-7. Both came out to do television stories about Abbas. Daniel Cohen's team won a regional Emmy Award for their story.

Abbas quickly ingratiated himself with the Fort Lauderdale community. Fort Lauderdale Mayor, Dean Trantalis, publicly declared July 20 Abbas Karimi Day and thanked him for representing our city in the Tokyo Paralympics. Members of our team were there to support him.

SOURCES

U.S. Paralympics Swimming:

U.S. Paralympics Swimming

www.paralympic.org/elizabeth-marks

Team USA website article about Abbas becoming a US citizen:
https://www.teamusa.org/News/2022/April/18/Para-Swimmer-Abbas-Karimi-Celebrating-Life-Career-In-United-States?fbclid=IwAR0MihNpAh7NKCs7FTca3se9P6UHcjbDwnmn1QmUwsXT4JQRngnZa1W0PhY

Swimming Bio:
https://www.paralympic.org/mohammad-abbas-karimi

Article:
https://www.paralympic.org/news/karimi-takes-long-and-winding-road-tokyo

New York Times article:
https://www.nytimes.com/2021/08/25/world/asia/afghan-swimmer-tokyo-paralympics.html?unlocked_article_code=1.40w.Suou.sdXrkDQXVcSW&smid=url-share

Video about the current crisis in Afghanistan:
https://www.nytimes.com/2023/02/27/world/asia/afghanistan-cold-malnutrition-crisis.html

Kabul history. The business of illegal drugs:
https://www.youtube.com/watch?v=TeEHOcC0Ruw

Angelina Jolie's interview with Abbas:
https://time.com/collection/time100-talks/?vid=2O52fl7J

Van, Turkey:
https://en.wikipedia.org/wiki/Van,_Turkey

What it is like to be smuggled into Turkey:
https://www.nytimes.com/2021/08/23/world/europe/afghanistan-refugees-turkey-iran-taliban-airport.html?action=click&module=RelatedLinks&pgtype=Article–

Traveling to Afghanistan now:
https://youtu.be/y2Nba4MMBAU?si=RC7ytfs28BStvc6b

The UNHCR Global Fundraising campaign:
donate.unhcr.org

The 2023 UNHCR Goodwill Ambassadors:
https://www.unhcr.org/us/about-unhcr/our-partners/prominent-supporters/goodwill-ambassadors

About the Department of Homeland Security:
https://www.dhs.gov/blog/2017/08/23/six-things-you-probably-didnt-know-about-uscis

ABOUT THE AUTHOR
Anita Mitchell

I am Anita Mitchell and I collect people stories, much the same way people collect shoes or baseball cards or Lladro porcelain figurines. During my 26 years at WSVN7, I had the front-row seat to people stories and it was there I learned about the extraordinariness of the ordinary…and the ordinariness of the extraordinary.

Since retiring from television news, I serve on the Board of Directors of Different Brains, a charitable foundation that supports neurodiverse adults. I also serve on the Board of Directors of the Broward County Sports Hall of Fame. We honor local residents who have set unique standards of excellence through sports.

I have a Communications/English BA from Michigan State University and was part of the Journalism masters program at Florida International University. I have one son, Randy Wagenheim, who lives in Tokyo, Japan.

Since 2004, I have swum competitively with our local Swim Fort Lauderdale Masters Swim Team (SFTL). I have a box full of ribbons and medals from swim meets. In both 2013 and 2017 I was a Team USA member for the Maccabi Games in Netanya, Israel.

I don't know how the writing and the swimming, the neurodiverse and honoring local sports figures are connected but I know in my heart that they are.

Printed in the USA
CPSIA information can be obtained
at www.ICGtesting.com
LVHW020152230324
775293LV00002B/4

9 798988 189152